S.P DEVDAS

the silent

Secret Mind Power of Meditation

Contents

1

Introduction to Meditation

Meditation is a timeless practice that has been embraced by cultures around the world for centuries. It's a journey inward, a practice of quieting the mind and focusing awareness on the present moment. At its core, meditation offers a sanctuary from the chaos of everyday life, providing a space for inner peace, reflection, and self-discovery.

In today's fast-paced world, where stress and distractions abound, meditation offers a powerful antidote. It invites us to slow down, to pause, and to reconnect with ourselves on a deeper level. While the practice of meditation may vary across different traditions and schools of thought, its essence remains universal: to cultivate mindfulness, awareness, and compassion.

Through meditation, we learn to observe our thoughts without judgment, to untangle ourselves from the grip of worry and anxiety, and to tap into a wellspring of inner calm and resilience. It's a practice that requires patience and persistence, but the rewards are profound.

In this journey of self-exploration, we'll explore the various forms of meditation, from mindfulness to transcendental meditation, and discover how each can enrich our lives in unique ways. Whether you're seeking relief from stress, a deeper connection with your inner self, or simply a moment of stillness in a chaotic world, meditation offers a path towards greater clarity, balance, and well-being.

Join us on this journey as we delve into the silent and secret mind power of meditation, unlocking its transformative potential and discovering the profound wisdom that lies within.

Meditation is a timeless practice that has been embraced by cultures and civilizations across the globe for centuries. It is a technique that allows individuals to cultivate a deeper sense of awareness, peace, and clarity by training the mind to focus and redirect thoughts. While the origins of meditation can be traced back to ancient spiritual traditions, its benefits have been recognized and studied by modern science, making it accessible to people from all walks of life.

At its core, meditation is about finding stillness within oneself amidst the chaos of everyday life. It involves consciously directing attention to the present moment, letting go of distractions and worries, and embracing a state of inner calm and tranquility. Through regular practice, meditation can help individuals reduce stress, improve concentration, enhance emotional well-being, and foster a greater sense of connection with oneself and others.

There are countless meditation techniques, ranging from mindfulness and breath awareness to visualization and mantra repetition. Each method offers its own unique benefits and approaches, allowing individuals to tailor their practice to suit their preferences and goals. Whether practiced in solitude or in a group setting, meditation offers a sanctuary for self-reflection and self-discovery, empowering individuals to tap into their inner wisdom and harness the power of the mind.

In this guide, we will explore the various aspects of meditation, from its rich history and scientific foundations to practical tips for starting and deepening your practice. Whether you are a beginner curious about meditation or an experienced practitioner seeking to deepen your understanding, this journey into the silent and secret mind power of meditation promises to be transformative and enlightening.

2

2

History and Origins of Meditation

Meditation, in various forms, has a rich and diverse history that spans thousands of years and encompasses numerous cultures and spiritual traditions. While pinpointing its exact origins can be challenging due to the vastness of time and the diversity of human experiences, archaeological evidence suggests that meditation practices date back to ancient civilizations such as those in India, China, and Mesopotamia.

One of the earliest documented records of meditation can be found in the teachings of Hinduism, which date back over 5,000 years. The ancient Indian scriptures known as the Vedas contain hymns and verses that describe meditation techniques aimed at achieving spiritual enlightenment and union with the divine. These early practices laid the foundation for what would later evolve into various forms of Hindu meditation, including Japa (repetition of mantras), Dhyana (focused concentration), and Raja Yoga (the royal path to self-realization).

In parallel, meditation also flourished in ancient China, particularly within the teachings of Taoism and Confucianism. Taoist meditation, rooted in the philosophical principles of balance and harmony, emphasized the cultivation of internal energy (Qi) and the alignment with the natural rhythms of the universe. Confucian meditation, on the other hand, focused on moral and ethical development through introspection and self-cultivation.

Around 500 BCE, the historical figure Siddhartha Gautama, later known as the Buddha, revolutionized the practice of meditation with his teachings on mindfulness and insight. After attaining enlightenment under the Bodhi tree, the Buddha introduced the Four Noble Truths and the Eightfold Path, which included meditation as a central component for overcoming suffering and achieving liberation from the cycle of birth and death (samsara).

Meditation also played a significant role in the development of other major world religions, including Jainism, Sikhism, and Christianity. In the Christian tradition, for example, practices such as contemplative prayer and Christian mysticism have roots in early monastic communities and the writings of mystics like St. Teresa of Avila and St. John of the Cross.

Throughout history, meditation has continued to evolve and adapt to different cultural contexts and spiritual beliefs. Today, it remains a universal practice embraced by people of diverse backgrounds, seeking inner peace, self-discovery, and spiritual fulfillment. As we delve deeper into the silent and secret mind power of meditation, it's essential to honor its rich history and the wisdom passed down through generations, guiding us on the path to greater understanding and enlightenment.

Meditation is a practice deeply rooted in the history of human civilization, with origins dating back thousands of years. While the precise origins of meditation are difficult to pinpoint due to its ancient and diverse roots, evidence suggests that meditation emerged independently in various cultures around the world.

One of the earliest recorded instances of meditation can be traced back to ancient India, where it was an integral part of Hindu spiritual practices. The ancient Indian scriptures known as the Vedas, composed around 1500 BCE, contain references to meditative techniques and the cultivation of inner stillness and awareness.

In the 6th century BCE, the teachings of Siddhartha Gautama, later known as the Buddha, further popularized meditation in India. The Buddha's emphasis on mindfulness, concentration, and insight meditation laid the foundation for what would become one of the central practices of Buddhism.

In parallel, meditation practices were also developing in other parts of the world. In ancient China, Taoist traditions emphasized meditation as a means of cultivating harmony with the natural world and achieving spiritual enlightenment. Taoist meditation techniques, such as Qigong and Tai Chi, continue to be practiced today for their health and spiritual benefits.

Similarly, in ancient Greece, philosophers such as Pythagoras and Plato advocated for contemplative practices aimed at achieving self-awareness and inner peace. These early Greek philosophical traditions laid the groundwork for later Western contemplative practices.

Throughout history, meditation has been woven into the fabric of religious and spiritual traditions around the world, including Christianity, Islam, Judaism, and Indigenous cultures. Whether through prayer, chanting, visualization, or silent contemplation, meditation has served as a means of connecting with the divine, exploring the nature of existence, and seeking inner transformation.

In the modern era, the practice of meditation has transcended its religious and cultural origins to become a widely studied and practiced technique for promoting physical, mental, and emotional well-being. Scientific research has confirmed the numerous benefits of meditation, leading to its integration into healthcare, education, and corporate settings.

As we delve deeper into the history and origins of meditation, we gain a deeper appreciation for its rich and diverse heritage, as well as its enduring relevance in today's fast-paced world. From ancient spiritual traditions to modern scientific inquiry, meditation continues to evolve as a powerful tool for self-discovery, healing, and personal growth.

The history of meditation is as diverse and ancient as human civilization itself. While its exact origins are difficult to pinpoint, evidence suggests that meditation practices emerged independently in various cultures across the globe, each with its own unique traditions and techniques.

One of the earliest recorded instances of meditation dates back to around 1500 BCE in ancient India, where it was integrated into the spiritual practices of Hinduism. The ancient Indian scriptures known as the Vedas contain references to meditative practices aimed at achieving states of heightened awareness and spiritual enlightenment. These early forms of meditation often involved deep concentration, breath control, and visualization techniques.

In the centuries that followed, meditation spread to other regions of Asia, including China and Japan, where it became an integral part of Taoist and Buddhist traditions. The teachings of Siddhartha Gautama, later known as the Buddha, emphasized meditation as a path to liberation from suffering and the attainment of enlightenment. Buddhist meditation practices, such as mindfulness and loving-kindness meditation, continue to be widely practiced and studied today.

Outside of Asia, meditation practices also flourished in ancient Greece, where philosophers like Pythagoras and Plato explored the concept of introspection and self-awareness. In the Christian tradition, contemplative prayer and meditation have been practiced since the early centuries of the Church, with notable figures such as Saint Augustine and Saint Teresa of Avila advocating for the importance of inner reflection and communion with the divine.

Throughout history, meditation has taken on many forms and been adapted to suit the cultural and religious beliefs of different societies. From the desert monasteries of Egypt to the mountaintop retreats of Tibet, meditation has been used as a tool for spiritual growth, self-discovery, and inner transformation.

In recent years, meditation has gained widespread popularity in the Western world, thanks in part to scientific research highlighting its numerous health benefits. Today, meditation is practiced by millions of people around the globe, transcending cultural and religious boundaries to become a universal means of finding peace, clarity, and purpose in an increasingly fast-paced and chaotic world.

3

3

Different Types of Meditation Practices

Meditation is a diverse practice with numerous techniques, each offering its own unique benefits and approaches. Whether you're seeking relaxation, self-awareness, or spiritual growth, there's likely a meditation practice suited to your preferences and goals. Here are some of the most common types of meditation:

1. **Mindfulness Meditation**: Mindfulness meditation involves paying attention to the present moment without judgment. Practitioners often focus on sensations like the breath, body, or sounds around them, bringing their awareness back to the present whenever the mind wanders.

2. **Breath Awareness Meditation**: This practice involves focusing on the breath as it enters and exits the body. By observing the rhythm of the breath, practitioners can cultivate a sense of calm and centeredness.

3. **Loving-Kindness Meditation**: Also known as Metta meditation, this practice involves cultivating feelings of love, compassion, and kindness towards oneself and others. Practitioners typically repeat phrases or mantras expressing well-wishes for themselves, loved ones, and even strangers.

4. **Transcendental Meditation (TM)**: TM is a technique where practitioners silently repeat a mantra, a word or phrase, to help focus the mind

9

and enter a state of deep relaxation and transcendence.

5. **Guided Meditation**: Guided meditation involves following the instructions of a teacher or recording that leads you through a series of visualizations or relaxation techniques. It's great for beginners or those who find it challenging to meditate on their own.

6. **Body Scan Meditation**: In this practice, practitioners systematically scan their body, paying attention to each part and noticing any sensations or tensions without judgment. It's a great way to cultivate body awareness and relaxation.

7. **Visualization Meditation**: Visualization involves imagining a peaceful scene, object, or scenario, and focusing on it with all the senses. This practice can help reduce stress and anxiety by creating a mental sanctuary.

8. **Mantra Meditation**: Similar to TM, mantra meditation involves repeating a sacred word or phrase to quiet the mind and induce a state of deep concentration and relaxation.

9. **Walking Meditation**: Instead of sitting still, walking meditation involves moving slowly and mindfully, paying attention to each step and the sensations in the body. It's a great way to incorporate mindfulness into daily activities.

10. **Chakra Meditation**: Based on ancient Hindu and Buddhist traditions, chakra meditation focuses on visualizing and balancing the body's energy centers (chakras) to promote physical, emotional, and spiritual well-being.

In recent decades, scientific research has increasingly explored the effects of meditation on the brain and body, revealing a wealth of evidence supporting its numerous health benefits. Advances in neuroscience and technology have allowed researchers to study the physiological and psychological effects of meditation in detail, shedding light on how this ancient practice can positively impact our well-being.

1. **Neuroplasticity**: One of the most significant findings in meditation research is its ability to promote neuroplasticity, the brain's capacity to reorganize and adapt in response to experiences and stimuli. Studies have shown that regular meditation practice can lead to structural changes in the brain, including increased gray matter density in regions associated with attention, memory, and emotional regulation.

2. **Stress Reduction**: Meditation has been extensively studied for its ability to reduce stress and promote relaxation. Research has shown that meditation techniques, such as mindfulness and deep breathing, can lower levels of cortisol, the body's primary stress hormone, and activate the parasympathetic nervous system, which induces a state of relaxation and calm.

3. **Emotional Regulation**: Meditation has been shown to enhance emotional regulation by strengthening the brain's prefrontal cortex, which is involved in decision-making, impulse control, and emotion regulation. Practitioners often report greater emotional resilience and a reduced tendency to react impulsively to stressful or challenging situations.

4. **Improved Cognitive Function**: Studies have found that meditation can enhance cognitive function, including attention, concentration, and memory. Mindfulness meditation, in particular, has been shown to improve sustained attention and cognitive flexibility, which are essential for tasks requiring mental focus and problem-solving.

5. **Pain Management**: Meditation has been found to be effective in reducing the perception of pain and increasing pain tolerance. Mindfulness-based interventions have been used successfully to alleviate chronic pain conditions, such as fibromyalgia, arthritis, and migraines, by promoting a non-judgmental awareness of pain sensations and reducing emotional reactivity to discomfort.

6. **Enhanced Well-Being**: Numerous studies have linked meditation to improvements in overall well-being, including greater feelings of happiness, contentment, and life satisfaction. Regular meditation practice has been associated with reduced symptoms of anxiety, depression, and other

mood disorders, as well as increased feelings of compassion, empathy, and connectedness with others.

7. **Immune Function**: Preliminary research suggests that meditation may have beneficial effects on immune function, with studies indicating that regular practice can enhance immune response and reduce inflammation. Meditation's stress-reducing effects may contribute to these immune-boosting benefits by reducing the body's inflammatory response to stress.

Overall, the scientific evidence supporting the benefits of meditation continues to grow, providing compelling reasons to incorporate this ancient practice into our modern lives. From reducing stress and enhancing emotional well-being to improving cognitive function and immune health, meditation offers a wealth of benefits for mind, body, and spirit, backed by rigorous scientific research.

4

4

The Science Behind Meditation

In recent decades, scientific research has increasingly explored the effects of meditation on the brain and body, revealing a wealth of evidence supporting its numerous health benefits. Advances in neuroscience and technology have allowed researchers to study the physiological and psychological effects of meditation in detail, shedding light on how this ancient practice can positively impact our well-being.

1. **Neuroplasticity**: One of the most significant findings in meditation research is its ability to promote neuroplasticity, the brain's capacity to reorganize and adapt in response to experiences and stimuli. Studies have shown that regular meditation practice can lead to structural changes in the brain, including increased gray matter density in regions associated with attention, memory, and emotional regulation.

2. **Stress Reduction**: Meditation has been extensively studied for its ability to reduce stress and promote relaxation. Research has shown that meditation techniques, such as mindfulness and deep breathing, can lower levels of cortisol, the body's primary stress hormone, and activate the parasympathetic nervous system, which induces a state of relaxation and calm.

3. **Emotional Regulation**: Meditation has been shown to enhance emotional regulation by strengthening the brain's prefrontal cortex,

which is involved in decision-making, impulse control, and emotion regulation. Practitioners often report greater emotional resilience and a reduced tendency to react impulsively to stressful or challenging situations.

4. **Improved Cognitive Function**: Studies have found that meditation can enhance cognitive function, including attention, concentration, and memory. Mindfulness meditation, in particular, has been shown to improve sustained attention and cognitive flexibility, which are essential for tasks requiring mental focus and problem-solving.

5. **Pain Management**: Meditation has been found to be effective in reducing the perception of pain and increasing pain tolerance. Mindfulness-based interventions have been used successfully to alleviate chronic pain conditions, such as fibromyalgia, arthritis, and migraines, by promoting a non-judgmental awareness of pain sensations and reducing emotional reactivity to discomfort.

6. **Enhanced Well-Being**: Numerous studies have linked meditation to improvements in overall well-being, including greater feelings of happiness, contentment, and life satisfaction. Regular meditation practice has been associated with reduced symptoms of anxiety, depression, and other mood disorders, as well as increased feelings of compassion, empathy, and connectedness with others.

7. **Immune Function**: Preliminary research suggests that meditation may have beneficial effects on immune function, with studies indicating that regular practice can enhance immune response and reduce inflammation. Meditation's stress-reducing effects may contribute to these immune-boosting benefits by reducing the body's inflammatory response to stress.

In recent decades, scientific research has provided compelling evidence of the numerous physical, mental, and emotional benefits of meditation. What was once considered a mystical or esoteric practice is now being studied and validated by researchers around the world. Here are some key findings from the scientific literature that shed light on the science behind meditation:

1. **Changes in Brain Structure**: Neuroimaging studies have shown that regular meditation practice can lead to structural changes in the brain, particularly in areas associated with attention, memory, emotional regulation, and self-awareness. These changes include increased gray matter density in the prefrontal cortex, hippocampus, and other regions involved in cognitive and emotional processing.

2. **Neuroplasticity**: Meditation has been found to promote neuroplasticity, the brain's ability to reorganize and adapt in response to experience. Through practices like mindfulness meditation, individuals can strengthen neural pathways associated with attention, compassion, and resilience, while weakening pathways linked to stress and anxiety.

3. **Stress Reduction**: One of the most well-documented benefits of meditation is its ability to reduce stress and promote relaxation. Studies have shown that meditation can lower levels of cortisol, the stress hormone, and activate the body's relaxation response, leading to decreased heart rate, blood pressure, and muscle tension.

4. **Emotional Regulation**: Meditation practices such as loving-kindness meditation have been found to enhance emotional regulation skills, allowing individuals to respond to challenging situations with greater equanimity and compassion. Research suggests that meditation can strengthen the connections between the prefrontal cortex and the amygdala, the brain's fear center, resulting in improved emotional resilience and well-being.

5. **Enhanced Attention and Concentration**: Meditation has been shown to improve attentional control and cognitive performance. By training the mind to focus and sustain attention on a single object or task, meditation can enhance concentration, working memory, and cognitive flexibility. These benefits have important implications for academic, professional, and everyday activities that require sustained mental effort.

6. **Pain Management**: Mindfulness meditation has been found to be effective in reducing the perception of pain and improving pain tolerance. Studies have shown that meditation can modulate pain processing in the brain, leading to decreased pain intensity and improved pain coping

strategies among individuals with chronic pain conditions.

7. **Improved Well-Being**: Beyond its effects on physical and mental health, meditation has been associated with greater overall well-being and quality of life. Research suggests that regular meditation practice can enhance feelings of happiness, gratitude, and life satisfaction, while reducing symptoms of depression, anxiety, and other mood disorders.

These findings provide compelling evidence of the profound impact that meditation can have on the brain, body, and mind. As scientists continue to unravel the mechanisms underlying meditation's therapeutic effects, its potential as a tool for promoting health, happiness, and resilience becomes increasingly clear.

5

5

Common Myths and Misconceptions About Meditation

Despite the growing popularity and scientific validation of meditation, several myths and misconceptions persist that can deter individuals from exploring this transformative practice. By debunking these myths, we can gain a clearer understanding of what meditation truly entails and its potential benefits. Here are some common myths and misconceptions about meditation:

1. **Meditation is only for spiritual or religious people**: While meditation has roots in various spiritual traditions, it is not inherently religious. Meditation can be practiced by people of all faiths or no faith at all. It is a secular practice that focuses on cultivating mindfulness, awareness, and inner peace, regardless of one's religious beliefs.

2. **You have to empty your mind completely**: One of the most common misconceptions about meditation is that you have to clear your mind of all thoughts to be successful. In reality, the goal of meditation is not to stop thinking altogether but to observe your thoughts without getting caught up in them. It's about cultivating a sense of presence and awareness rather than achieving a state of mental emptiness.

3. **You need to meditate for hours to experience benefits**: While longer

meditation sessions can be beneficial, even just a few minutes of daily practice can yield significant benefits. Consistency is key, so focusing on establishing a regular meditation routine is more important than the length of each session. Short, frequent sessions can be just as effective as longer ones.

4. **Meditation is only for people who are calm and relaxed**: Some people believe that they need to be in a calm or relaxed state to meditate effectively. However, meditation can be practiced at any time, regardless of your current emotional state. In fact, meditation can be especially helpful during times of stress, anxiety, or agitation, as it provides a tool for managing and coping with difficult emotions.

5. **You have to sit cross-legged on the floor to meditate**: While the stereotypical image of meditation often involves sitting cross-legged on a cushion, there are many different ways to meditate. You can meditate while sitting in a chair, lying down, standing, or even walking. The most important thing is to find a comfortable and stable position that allows you to maintain alertness and relaxation.

6. **Meditation is a quick fix for all problems**: While meditation can have profound benefits for mental, emotional, and physical well-being, it is not a panacea for all problems. Like any skill, meditation requires time, patience, and practice to develop. While it can be a valuable tool for managing stress, improving focus, and enhancing self-awareness, it is not a substitute for professional medical or psychological treatment when needed.

Despite its growing popularity and widespread acceptance, meditation is still surrounded by various myths and misconceptions. These misconceptions can sometimes discourage people from trying meditation or lead to unrealistic expectations about its benefits. Here are some common myths and misconceptions about meditation:

1. **You have to clear your mind completely**: One of the most prevalent myths about meditation is that you need to completely clear your mind

of thoughts in order to meditate successfully. In reality, the goal of meditation is not to stop thinking altogether but rather to observe your thoughts without judgment and gently redirect your attention when you become distracted.

2. **Meditation is only for spiritual or religious people**: While meditation has roots in various spiritual and religious traditions, it is not inherently tied to any specific belief system. Meditation can be practiced by people of all faiths or no faith at all, and its benefits are accessible to anyone regardless of their spiritual or religious background.

3. **You need a lot of time to meditate**: Another common misconception is that meditation requires long periods of time to be effective. While longer meditation sessions can certainly be beneficial, even just a few minutes of daily practice can yield noticeable benefits. It's more important to prioritize consistency and regularity in your practice than the length of each session.

4. **Meditation is only for experienced yogis or monks**: Some people may believe that meditation is only for experienced practitioners who have dedicated their lives to spiritual pursuits. In reality, meditation is a skill that anyone can learn and benefit from, regardless of their level of experience or expertise.

5. **Meditation is about escaping reality**: Another misconception is that meditation is about escaping from reality or avoiding life's challenges. On the contrary, meditation is about cultivating awareness and acceptance of the present moment, including both its joys and its difficulties. Through meditation, we learn to respond to life's ups and downs with greater clarity, equanimity, and resilience.

6. **You have to sit in a specific posture**: While traditional meditation postures like sitting cross-legged on the floor can be beneficial for some people, they are not necessary for everyone. The most important thing is to find a comfortable and sustainable posture that allows you to remain alert and relaxed throughout your practice. You can meditate while sitting in a chair, lying down, or even walking.

7. **Meditation is a quick fix for all problems**: While meditation can

offer numerous benefits for physical, mental, and emotional well-being, it is not a magical cure-all for every problem. Like any skill or practice, meditation requires time, patience, and dedication to yield meaningful results. It can be a powerful tool for personal growth and transformation, but it is not a substitute for professional medical or psychological treatment when needed.

By dispelling these common myths and misconceptions, we can create a more accurate understanding of what meditation is and how it can be integrated into our lives as a practical and accessible tool for self-care and self-discovery.

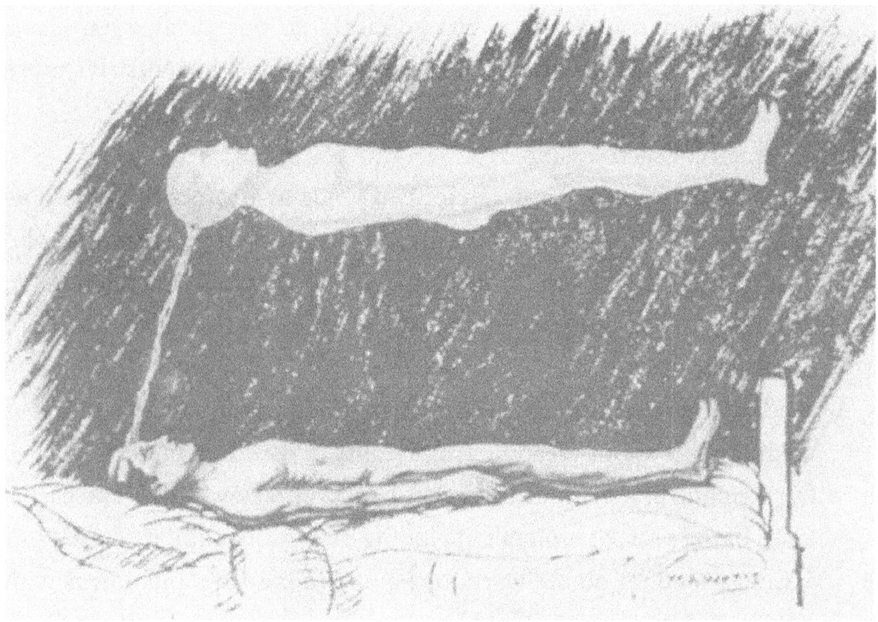

6

6

The Mind-Body Connection

The mind-body connection refers to the intricate relationship between our mental and physical health, highlighting the ways in which our thoughts, emotions, beliefs, and attitudes can influence our physical well-being, and vice versa. This concept underscores the interconnectedness of the mind and body, suggesting that changes in one can have profound effects on the other.

1. **Effects of Stress on the Body**: One of the most well-documented examples of the mind-body connection is the impact of stress on physical health. Chronic stress can lead to a range of physical health problems, including high blood pressure, weakened immune function, digestive issues, and cardiovascular disease. This occurs through the release of stress hormones like cortisol, which can disrupt the body's natural balance and contribute to inflammation and disease.

2. **Psychosomatic Illnesses**: Psychosomatic illnesses are conditions that have both psychological and physical components, with symptoms that are influenced by emotional or mental factors. Examples include tension headaches, irritable bowel syndrome, and chronic pain conditions like fibromyalgia. By addressing underlying psychological stressors or emotional conflicts, individuals may experience improvements in their physical symptoms.

3. **Placebo Effect**: The placebo effect is another manifestation of the mind-body connection, demonstrating the power of belief and expectation in shaping our health outcomes. Research has shown that patients who receive a placebo treatment often experience real improvements in their symptoms, simply because they believe they are receiving an effective intervention. This highlights the role of the mind in influencing the body's healing processes.

4. **Mindfulness and Pain Management**: Practices like mindfulness meditation have been shown to be effective in managing chronic pain by changing the way the brain perceives and responds to pain signals. By cultivating present-moment awareness and non-judgmental acceptance of pain sensations, individuals can reduce their experience of pain and improve their quality of life.

5. **Emotional Health and Immune Function**: There is growing evidence to suggest that emotional well-being and immune function are closely linked. Negative emotions like stress, anxiety, and depression can weaken the immune system, making individuals more susceptible to infections and illnesses. Conversely, positive emotions like happiness, optimism, and gratitude have been associated with enhanced immune function and better overall health.

6. **Mind-Body Interventions**: Recognizing the profound influence of the mind on physical health, an increasing number of healthcare providers are incorporating mind-body interventions into their treatment plans. These interventions, which may include techniques like meditation, yoga, tai chi, and biofeedback, aim to harness the body's natural healing abilities and promote holistic well-being.

Overall, the mind-body connection highlights the complex interplay between our mental and physical states and underscores the importance of addressing both aspects of our health for optimal well-being. By cultivating a greater awareness of this connection and adopting practices that support harmony between the mind and body, individuals can empower themselves to lead healthier, more balanced lives.

The mind-body connection refers to the intricate relationship between our thoughts, emotions, beliefs, and physical health. It suggests that our mental and emotional states can significantly impact our physical well-being, and vice versa. This concept has been recognized by ancient healing traditions for centuries and is now supported by scientific research.

1. **Emotions and Physical Health**: Our emotions, such as stress, anxiety, and happiness, can have profound effects on our physical health. Chronic stress, for example, is associated with a wide range of health problems, including high blood pressure, weakened immune function, and digestive disorders. Conversely, positive emotions like joy and gratitude can boost immune function, reduce inflammation, and promote overall well-being.

2. **The Stress Response**: When we experience stress, whether it's from external sources like work or relationships or internal sources like negative thoughts and worries, our bodies initiate the "fight-or-flight" response. This triggers a cascade of physiological changes, including the release of stress hormones like cortisol and adrenaline, increased heart rate, and heightened muscle tension. Chronic activation of the stress response can contribute to a variety of health issues, highlighting the importance of managing stress through practices like meditation, mindfulness, and relaxation techniques.

3. **Psychoneuroimmunology**: Psychoneuroimmunology is the study of how psychological factors, such as stress and emotions, influence the immune system and overall health. Research in this field has demonstrated that psychological stress can weaken immune function, making individuals more susceptible to infections and diseases. Conversely, positive psychological states, such as optimism and resilience, are associated with enhanced immune function and better health outcomes.

4. **Placebo Effect**: The placebo effect is a phenomenon in which a person experiences improvements in symptoms or outcomes after receiving a treatment that has no therapeutic effect. This suggests that our beliefs, expectations, and perceptions play a significant role in our response

to medical interventions. The placebo effect highlights the powerful influence of the mind on the body's healing processes and underscores the importance of harnessing the mind-body connection in medical care.

5. **Mind-Body Practices**: Mind-body practices like meditation, yoga, tai chi, and qigong are increasingly recognized for their ability to promote health and well-being by strengthening the mind-body connection. These practices combine physical movement, breathwork, and mental focus to cultivate relaxation, reduce stress, and enhance overall vitality. Research has shown that mind-body practices can have beneficial effects on various health conditions, including chronic pain, anxiety, depression, and cardiovascular disease.

Understanding and nurturing the mind-body connection is essential for achieving optimal health and well-being. By cultivating awareness of how our thoughts, emotions, and behaviors influence our physical health, we can empower ourselves to make positive changes that support holistic wellness and vitality.

7

7

Creating a Meditation Space

Designing a dedicated meditation space can greatly enhance the quality of your meditation practice by providing a tranquil environment conducive to relaxation and inner reflection. Whether you have a whole room to spare or just a small corner of your home, here are some tips for creating your own meditation sanctuary:

1. **Choose a Quiet Location**: Select a quiet and peaceful location in your home where you're least likely to be disturbed. This could be a spare room, a corner of your bedroom, or even a secluded spot in your garden. Minimize distractions by choosing a space away from noisy appliances, electronic devices, and high-traffic areas.

2. **Keep it Clean and Clutter-Free**: A cluttered environment can create mental clutter and detract from your meditation experience. Keep your meditation space clean, tidy, and free from unnecessary distractions. Consider using minimal decor and furnishings to create a sense of spaciousness and tranquility.

3. **Set the Mood with Lighting**: Lighting plays a crucial role in setting the mood for meditation. Choose soft, diffused lighting that creates a warm and inviting atmosphere. Consider using candles, Himalayan salt lamps, or dimmable LED lights to create a soft glow that promotes relaxation and focus.

4. **Add Comfortable Seating**: Choose comfortable seating options that support good posture and relaxation. This could be a cushioned meditation cushion (zafu), a meditation bench, or a comfortable chair with good back support. Experiment with different seating arrangements to find what works best for you.

5. **Incorporate Natural Elements**: Bring elements of nature into your meditation space to create a sense of serenity and connection with the natural world. This could include potted plants, fresh flowers, natural materials like wood or stone, or a small indoor fountain or waterfall.

6. **Personalize Your Space**: Infuse your meditation space with personal touches that reflect your tastes, interests, and spiritual beliefs. Display meaningful objects like crystals, statues, or sacred symbols that inspire and uplift you. Surround yourself with items that evoke a sense of peace, gratitude, and mindfulness.

7. **Create Ambiance with Scent**: Aromatherapy can enhance the ambiance of your meditation space and promote relaxation. Experiment with essential oils or incense sticks in calming scents like lavender, sandalwood, or frankincense. Use a diffuser or incense holder to disperse the scent gently throughout the room.

8. **Limit Electronic Devices**: Minimize the presence of electronic devices in your meditation space to reduce distractions and maintain a sense of tranquility. Consider setting boundaries around screen time and creating designated tech-free zones in your home to support your mindfulness practice.

By creating a dedicated meditation space tailored to your preferences and needs, you can establish a sacred sanctuary where you can retreat to cultivate inner peace, clarity, and mindfulness. Whether it's a small corner of your home or a dedicated meditation room, your meditation space should be a reflection of your commitment to self-care and spiritual growth.

Designing a dedicated meditation space can significantly enhance the quality and effectiveness of your meditation practice. Here are some tips for creating a tranquil and inspiring meditation space:

1. **Choose a Quiet Location**: Select a quiet and peaceful location in your home where you can practice meditation without distractions. Ideally, choose a space away from noisy areas and household traffic to create a sense of calm and serenity.

2. **Clear the Clutter**: Remove any clutter or unnecessary items from your meditation space to create a clean and uncluttered environment. A clutter-free space can help promote mental clarity and focus during meditation.

3. **Set the Mood with Lighting**: Consider the lighting in your meditation space and aim for soft, natural lighting whenever possible. You can use candles, string lights, or dimmable lamps to create a warm and inviting atmosphere conducive to relaxation and introspection.

4. **Add Comfortable Seating**: Choose a comfortable seating option that supports an upright posture and allows you to sit comfortably for an extended period. Options include meditation cushions (zafus), yoga mats, or a comfortable chair with good back support.

5. **Incorporate Natural Elements**: Bring elements of nature into your meditation space to create a sense of connection with the natural world. This could include plants, flowers, rocks, or a small indoor fountain to evoke a peaceful and grounding ambiance.

6. **Personalize Your Space**: Add personal touches to your meditation space to make it feel uniquely yours. This could include meaningful artwork, inspirational quotes, or objects that hold special significance to you. Surrounding yourself with items that bring you joy and inspiration can enhance your meditation experience.

7. **Create a Sacred Altar or Focal Point**: Consider creating a sacred altar or focal point in your meditation space where you can display meaningful objects or symbols that represent your spiritual or personal intentions. This could include candles, incense, crystals, or religious icons that inspire reflection and contemplation.

8. **Keep it Clean and Tidy**: Regularly clean and maintain your meditation space to keep it fresh and inviting. Take a few moments before each meditation session to tidy up the space and remove any distractions or

clutter that may detract from your practice.

By creating a dedicated meditation space that is comfortable, peaceful, and conducive to inner reflection, you can establish a supportive environment for your meditation practice and deepen your connection to yourself and the present moment.

8

8

The Importance of Posture in Meditation

Posture plays a crucial role in meditation, as it affects both the physical comfort and the mental clarity of the practitioner. Here's why posture is important in meditation:

1. **Physical Comfort**: A proper meditation posture helps minimize discomfort and physical distractions during meditation. Sitting with an upright spine reduces the likelihood of back pain, stiffness, and discomfort that can arise from slouching or improper alignment. When the body is relaxed and comfortable, it's easier to maintain focus and concentration during meditation.

2. **Optimal Breathing**: Good posture facilitates optimal breathing, which is essential for deepening relaxation and calming the mind during meditation. When the spine is aligned and the chest is open, the breath can flow freely and effortlessly, allowing for deep, diaphragmatic breathing. This type of breathing activates the body's relaxation response and promotes a sense of calm and inner peace.

3. **Enhanced Alertness**: Sitting with an upright posture promotes alertness and wakefulness during meditation. When the spine is erect and the shoulders are relaxed, energy can flow freely throughout the body, helping to keep the mind alert and focused. Slumping or slouching, on the other hand, can lead to lethargy and drowsiness, making it more

difficult to maintain mental clarity and awareness.

4. **Alignment of Energy Centers**: According to yoga and traditional Chinese medicine, proper posture helps align the body's energy centers, or chakras, which are believed to play a role in physical, mental, and emotional well-being. Sitting with a straight spine and an open heart center can facilitate the flow of energy throughout the body, promoting balance, harmony, and vitality.

5. **Mind-Body Connection**: The way we hold our bodies can influence our mental and emotional states. By adopting a posture of strength, stability, and openness during meditation, we can cultivate a sense of confidence, resilience, and inner peace. Conversely, slouched or collapsed posture can contribute to feelings of insecurity, low energy, and agitation.

6. **Mindfulness and Awareness**: Maintaining an upright posture encourages mindfulness and self-awareness during meditation. As we sit with intention and awareness of our body alignment, we become more attuned to physical sensations, thoughts, and emotions that arise during meditation. This heightened awareness can deepen our understanding of ourselves and our inner landscape.

In summary, proper posture is essential for creating a supportive foundation for meditation practice. By sitting with an upright spine, relaxed shoulders, and an open heart, we can enhance physical comfort, optimize breathing, promote mental clarity, and cultivate mindfulness and self-awareness. Through consistent attention to posture, we can harness the power of the mind-body connection to deepen our meditation practice and access greater states of peace, presence, and well-being.

Posture plays a crucial role in meditation, as it directly influences your physical comfort, mental alertness, and overall ability to maintain focus and concentration. Here's why posture is important in meditation:

1. **Physical Comfort**: Maintaining a comfortable and stable posture during meditation helps minimize physical discomfort and distractions, allowing you to sit for longer periods without experiencing discomfort

or pain. Proper posture ensures that your body is properly aligned and supported, reducing strain on your muscles and joints.

2. **Optimal Breathing**: Good posture promotes optimal breathing by allowing your lungs to expand fully and your diaphragm to move freely. When you sit with an upright spine and open chest, you can breathe more deeply and effortlessly, facilitating relaxation and stress reduction.

3. **Mental Alertness**: Posture can influence your level of mental alertness and wakefulness during meditation. Sitting with a straight spine and lifted chest encourages a sense of wakefulness and attentiveness, helping you stay focused and present throughout your meditation practice.

4. **Energy Flow**: According to traditional yogic and Chinese medicine principles, proper posture facilitates the smooth flow of energy (prana or qi) throughout the body. When you sit with a tall spine and relaxed shoulders, energy can flow freely through the subtle energy channels (nadis or meridians), promoting vitality and well-being.

5. **Mind-Body Connection**: Your posture reflects and influences your mental and emotional state. By sitting with an upright and dignified posture, you convey a sense of confidence, openness, and inner strength. This posture can help cultivate a positive mindset and a deeper sense of self-awareness during meditation.

6. **Mindfulness and Presence**: Maintaining awareness of your posture during meditation can enhance your mindfulness practice. By paying attention to the sensations of sitting, the alignment of your spine, and the subtle movements of your body, you deepen your connection to the present moment and cultivate greater self-awareness.

7. **Symbolic Meaning**: In many spiritual traditions, posture carries symbolic significance and represents qualities such as stability, balance, and inner strength. Sitting with a grounded and upright posture reflects a commitment to inner growth and spiritual development, embodying qualities of resilience and equanimity.

In conclusion, paying attention to your posture during meditation is essential for creating a supportive and conducive environment for your practice. By sitting with a comfortable, stable, and dignified posture, you can enhance your physical comfort, mental clarity, and overall meditation experience.

9

Breathing Techniques for Meditation

Breath is the foundation of meditation practice, serving as a focal point for attention and a gateway to deeper states of awareness and relaxation. Here are some commonly practiced breathing techniques used in meditation:

1. **Deep Belly Breathing (Diaphragmatic Breathing)**: This technique involves breathing deeply into the lower abdomen, allowing the diaphragm to expand fully. Start by inhaling slowly through your nose, allowing your belly to rise as you fill your lungs with air. Exhale gently through your nose or mouth, letting your belly fall as you release the breath. Deep belly breathing promotes relaxation, reduces stress, and enhances oxygen flow to the body and brain.

2. **Equal Breathing (Sama Vritti)**: In equal breathing, the inhalation and exhalation are of equal duration. Start by inhaling deeply for a count of four, then exhale for a count of four. Repeat this cycle for several breaths, gradually extending the duration if comfortable. Equal breathing helps balance the nervous system, calm the mind, and promote focus and concentration.

3. **4-7-8 Breathing (Relaxing Breath)**: This technique involves inhaling for a count of four, holding the breath for a count of seven, and exhaling

for a count of eight. Start by exhaling completely through your mouth, then inhale quietly through your nose for four counts. Hold your breath for seven counts, then exhale slowly through your mouth for eight counts. Repeat this cycle several times. 4-7-8 breathing is effective for inducing relaxation, reducing anxiety, and promoting restful sleep.

4. **Alternate Nostril Breathing (Nadi Shodhana)**: Nadi Shodhana is a yogic breathing technique that involves alternating between the left and right nostrils. Start by closing your right nostril with your thumb and inhaling deeply through your left nostril. Then close your left nostril with your ring finger and exhale through your right nostril. Inhale through your right nostril, then close it and exhale through your left nostril. Continue alternating nostrils for several breaths. Nadi Shodhana balances the flow of energy in the body, clears the mind, and promotes mental clarity.

5. **Box Breathing (Square Breathing)**: Box breathing involves inhaling, holding the breath, exhaling, and holding the breath again, all for equal counts. Start by inhaling deeply for a count of four, then hold your breath for a count of four. Exhale slowly for a count of four, then hold your breath again for a count of four. Repeat this cycle several times, visualizing a square with each breath. Box breathing promotes relaxation, reduces stress, and increases focus and awareness.

6. **Guided Visualization**: In this technique, you use your imagination to visualize your breath as a flowing stream or a glowing light. As you inhale, imagine breathing in peace, joy, or healing energy. As you exhale, imagine releasing tension, negativity, or stress. Guided visualization enhances relaxation, fosters creativity, and deepens the mind-body connection.

Breath is a fundamental aspect of meditation, serving as a focal point for attention and a gateway to deeper states of awareness and relaxation. Here are some common breathing techniques used in meditation:

1. **Deep Belly Breathing (Diaphragmatic Breathing)**: This technique involves breathing deeply into the abdomen, allowing the diaphragm to expand fully. To practice deep belly breathing, inhale deeply through your nose, allowing your abdomen to rise as you fill your lungs with air. Exhale slowly and completely through your nose or mouth, allowing your abdomen to fall. Focus on the sensation of your breath moving in and out of your body, and allow each breath to be slow, deep, and natural.

2. **Equal Breathing (Sama Vritti)**: In equal breathing, you inhale and exhale for an equal count, creating a balanced rhythm of breath. Start by inhaling for a count of four, then exhale for a count of four. As you become more comfortable with this rhythm, you can gradually increase the duration of each inhale and exhale. Equal breathing helps to calm the mind, reduce stress, and promote relaxation.

3. **Counting Breaths**: Counting breaths is a simple yet effective technique for maintaining focus and concentration during meditation. To practice, silently count each breath as you inhale and exhale. Start with a count of one on the inhale, then two on the exhale, and continue counting up to five or ten breaths. If your mind wanders, gently bring your attention back to the count, starting again from one.

4. **Alternate Nostril Breathing (Nadi Shodhana)**: Nadi Shodhana is a pranayama (breath control) technique that involves alternating between the left and right nostrils. To practice, use your right thumb to close your right nostril and inhale deeply through your left nostril. Then, use your right ring finger to close your left nostril and exhale through your right nostril. Inhale through the right nostril, then close it with your thumb and exhale through the left nostril. Continue alternating nostrils for several breaths. Nadi Shodhana helps balance the flow of energy in the body and promotes mental clarity.

5. **Ujjayi Breathing**: Ujjayi breath, also known as "ocean breath" or "victorious breath," involves constricting the back of the throat to create a gentle hissing sound during both inhalation and exhalation. To practice ujjayi breathing, inhale deeply through your nose while slightly

contracting the back of your throat, then exhale slowly and audibly through your nose, maintaining the constriction in the throat. Ujjayi breath helps to calm the mind, regulate the nervous system, and deepen your meditation practice.

6. **Guided Visualization with Breath**: In guided visualization, you can combine breath awareness with imagery to deepen relaxation and promote inner peace. As you inhale, visualize breathing in positive energy, light, or healing energy. As you exhale, imagine releasing tension, stress, or negative emotions. Allow each inhale to energize and uplift you, and each exhale to cleanse and purify your mind and body.

Experiment with these breathing techniques to discover which ones resonate most with you and support your meditation practice. By cultivating awareness of your breath and incorporating intentional breathing into your meditation routine, you can enhance your ability to relax, focus, and connect with the present moment.

10

10

Mantras and Affirmations in Meditation

Mantras and affirmations are powerful tools used in meditation to focus the mind, cultivate positive energy, and promote self-awareness and personal growth. Here's how you can incorporate mantras and affirmations into your meditation practice:

1. **Understanding Mantras**: A mantra is a sacred sound, word, or phrase that is repeated silently or aloud during meditation to aid in concentration and spiritual growth. Mantras can be traditional Sanskrit chants, such as "Om" or "So Hum," or they can be simple affirmations in your native language. The repetition of a mantra creates a rhythmic vibration that helps quiet the mind and deepen your meditation experience.

2. **Choosing a Mantra or Affirmation**: When choosing a mantra or affirmation for meditation, consider selecting a word or phrase that resonates with your intentions, values, or spiritual beliefs. It could be a word that embodies qualities you wish to cultivate, such as "peace," "love," "gratitude," or "strength." Alternatively, you can create your own affirmations that reflect your personal goals, aspirations, or values.

3. **Repeating the Mantra**: Once you have chosen a mantra or affirmation, sit comfortably in a quiet space and begin repeating it silently or aloud. You can synchronize the repetition of the mantra with your breath,

inhaling as you silently say the first part of the mantra and exhaling as you say the second part. Alternatively, you can repeat the mantra at your own pace, focusing your attention on the sound and vibration of each syllable.

4. **Staying Present and Focused**: As you repeat the mantra or affirmation, allow your mind to become fully absorbed in the sound and meaning of the words. If your mind wanders or becomes distracted, gently bring your attention back to the mantra, using it as an anchor to stay present and focused. Notice any sensations, emotions, or thoughts that arise during the practice, and allow them to come and go without judgment.

5. **Deepening the Practice**: As you become more comfortable with the practice of mantra meditation, you can experiment with different techniques to deepen your experience. You may choose to vary the speed or intensity of the repetition, or incorporate visualization or movement into your practice. The key is to find a method that resonates with you and supports your journey of self-discovery and spiritual growth.

6. **Integrating Affirmations into Daily Life**: In addition to using affirmations during meditation, you can also incorporate them into your daily life as a tool for positive thinking and self-empowerment. Repeat your affirmations regularly, either silently or aloud, to reinforce positive beliefs and intentions and overcome negative self-talk or limiting beliefs.

Mantras and affirmations are powerful tools used in meditation to focus the mind, cultivate positive energy, and promote inner transformation. Here's how you can incorporate mantras and affirmations into your meditation practice:

1. **Choosing a Mantra or Affirmation**: A mantra is a sacred word, phrase, or sound that is repeated silently or aloud during meditation to invoke a specific quality or state of consciousness. An affirmation is a positive statement or phrase that reinforces a desired belief or intention. When choosing a mantra or affirmation, select words or phrases that resonate with you and align with your intentions for meditation. This could be

a traditional Sanskrit mantra, such as "Om" or "So Hum," or a simple affirmation like "I am peaceful" or "I am enough."

2. **Repeating the Mantra or Affirmation**: Once you have chosen your mantra or affirmation, begin your meditation by silently repeating it in your mind or softly chanting it aloud. Allow the words to resonate within you, feeling their vibration and energy permeate your being. Focus your attention on the sound, meaning, and feeling of the mantra or affirmation, letting go of any distractions or wandering thoughts.

3. **Syncing with the Breath**: You can synchronize your mantra or affirmation with your breath to enhance its effectiveness. For example, as you inhale, silently repeat the first half of your mantra or affirmation, and as you exhale, repeat the second half. This rhythmic repetition helps anchor your attention and deepen your state of relaxation and focus.

4. **Visualizing the Mantra or Affirmation**: Another way to deepen your connection to your mantra or affirmation is to visualize it as you repeat it. Imagine the words or phrases glowing with light or radiating positive energy throughout your body and mind. Visualizing your mantra or affirmation can amplify its effects and make it feel more tangible and real.

5. **Letting Go of Attachments**: As you repeat your mantra or affirmation, allow yourself to let go of any attachment to specific outcomes or experiences. Instead, cultivate a sense of surrender and trust in the power of the mantra or affirmation to guide and support you on your journey. Trust that the repeated repetition of these words will gradually shift your mindset and consciousness in positive ways.

6. **Reflecting on the Meaning**: After your meditation session, take a few moments to reflect on the meaning and significance of your chosen mantra or affirmation. Notice any shifts in your thoughts, emotions, or energy levels, and observe how your practice influences your state of mind and overall well-being.

By incorporating mantras and affirmations into your meditation practice, you can harness the power of sound and intention to deepen your connection to yourself, cultivate positive qualities, and enhance your overall sense of inner peace and fulfillment.

11

11

Setting Intentions in Meditation

Setting intentions is a powerful practice that can help you clarify your goals, align your actions with your values, and cultivate a sense of purpose and direction in your life. When incorporated into meditation, setting intentions can deepen your practice and enhance your ability to manifest positive changes. Here's how you can set intentions in meditation:

1. **Reflect on Your Values and Desires**: Begin by taking some time to reflect on what matters most to you and what you hope to achieve or cultivate in your life. Consider your values, aspirations, and long-term goals, as well as any areas of your life where you would like to see growth or transformation.

2. **Choose a Clear and Specific Intention**: Once you have identified your values and desires, choose a clear and specific intention that reflects what you want to manifest or cultivate. Your intention could be related to personal growth, relationships, career, health, or any other aspect of your life. Make sure your intention is positive, empowering, and aligned with your highest good.

3. **Phrase Your Intention Affirmatively**: Frame your intention in positive, affirming language, as if it is already happening or has already been achieved. For example, instead of saying "I want to be less stressed,"

rephrase it as "I am calm, centered, and at peace." This helps to shift your mindset from one of lack or need to one of abundance and possibility.

4. **Visualize Your Intention Coming to Fruition**: Once you have formulated your intention, take a few moments to visualize it as if it has already been realized. Imagine yourself living your intention fully and experiencing the feelings, sensations, and outcomes associated with it. Visualization can help reinforce your intention and activate the creative power of your subconscious mind.

5. **Repeat Your Intention During Meditation**: During your meditation practice, incorporate your intention by silently repeating it in your mind or softly chanting it aloud. Allow the words of your intention to resonate within you, infusing your consciousness with the energy and vibration of your desired outcome. You can synchronize the repetition of your intention with your breath to deepen your focus and concentration.

6. **Release Attachments and Surrender to the Outcome**: After stating your intention, let go of any attachment to specific outcomes or expectations. Trust that the universe has heard your intention and is working to bring it to fruition in its own time and way. Practice surrendering to the process and remaining open to the infinite possibilities that may unfold.

7. **Act in Alignment with Your Intention**: Finally, carry the energy of your intention with you beyond your meditation practice by taking inspired action in alignment with your goals and values. Notice opportunities and synchronicities that arise in support of your intention, and be proactive in pursuing them with confidence and clarity.

Setting intentions is a powerful practice that helps focus your energy and attention on specific goals or aspirations during meditation. Here's how you can set intentions and incorporate them into your meditation practice:

1. **Reflect on Your Purpose**: Before you begin your meditation, take a moment to reflect on your purpose or reason for practicing. Ask yourself what you hope to achieve or experience during your meditation session.

Your intention could be anything from cultivating inner peace and clarity to fostering compassion or gratitude.

2. **Clarify Your Intention**: Once you have identified your general intention, take some time to clarify and refine it into a concise statement or affirmation. Your intention should be positive, present-tense, and aligned with your values and aspirations. For example, "I cultivate compassion towards myself and others" or "I embrace a sense of calm and centeredness."

3. **Set Your Intention**: With your intention in mind, set it consciously at the beginning of your meditation session. You can do this by silently repeating your intention as a mantra, visualizing it as a guiding light or energy, or simply stating it aloud as a declaration of your commitment. Allow yourself to connect deeply with your intention, feeling its resonance within you.

4. **Anchor Your Intention with Breath**: As you settle into your meditation, synchronize your breath with your intention to anchor it more deeply into your awareness. With each inhale, breathe in the energy and essence of your intention, feeling it permeate every cell of your being. With each exhale, release any resistance or distractions, allowing your intention to take root and grow stronger within you.

5. **Stay Present with Your Intention**: Throughout your meditation practice, keep your intention at the forefront of your awareness. Whenever your mind begins to wander or stray, gently bring your attention back to your intention, using it as a focal point to anchor your mind and cultivate presence. Notice how your intention influences your thoughts, emotions, and overall state of being.

6. **Release Attachment to Outcomes**: While it's natural to have desires and expectations associated with your intention, try to release attachment to specific outcomes or experiences. Instead, focus on embodying the qualities and values inherent in your intention, trusting that the process of meditation will unfold in its own time and way.

7. **Express Gratitude**: At the end of your meditation session, take a moment to express gratitude for the opportunity to practice and for

the guidance and support of your intention. Reflect on any insights or experiences that arose during your meditation, and acknowledge the progress you've made towards embodying your intention in your daily life.

By setting intentions in your meditation practice, you can harness the power of focused attention and intention to cultivate positive qualities, align with your deepest values, and manifest your aspirations with greater clarity and purpose.

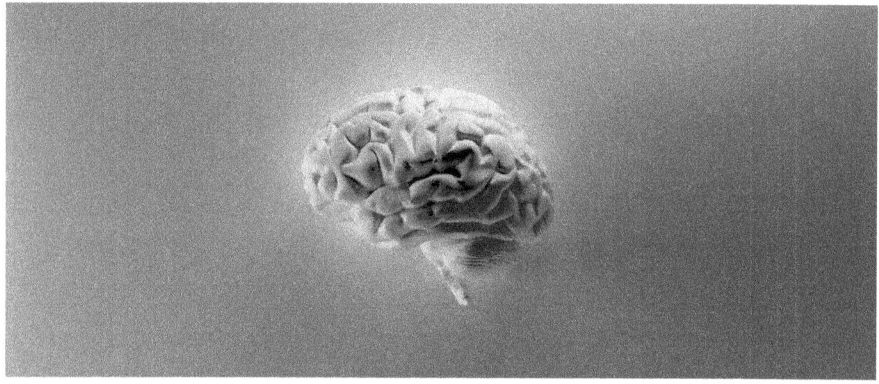

12

12

Starting Simple: Guided Meditations

Guided meditations are an excellent way for beginners to ease into the practice of meditation. These structured sessions provide step-by-step instructions and verbal guidance to help you relax, focus your mind, and deepen your awareness. Here's how you can start simple with guided meditations:

1. **Find a Comfortable Position**: Begin by finding a comfortable position for meditation, either sitting on a cushion or chair with your back straight and your hands resting comfortably in your lap. You can also lie down if that's more comfortable for you. Close your eyes gently and take a few deep breaths to relax your body and mind.

2. **Choose a Guided Meditation**: There are countless guided meditation recordings available online, ranging from basic relaxation exercises to more specific practices like mindfulness, loving-kindness, or body scan meditations. Choose a guided meditation that resonates with you and aligns with your intentions for your practice.

3. **Follow the Instructions**: Once you've selected a guided meditation, press play and listen to the instructions provided by the guide. The guide will likely lead you through a series of relaxation techniques, breath awareness exercises, and visualizations designed to help you enter a state of deep relaxation and inner peace.

4. **Focus on the Guidance**: As you listen to the guide's voice, allow yourself to surrender to their instructions and follow along with an open mind and heart. Pay attention to the sensations in your body, the rhythm of your breath, and any thoughts or emotions that arise without judgment or attachment.

5. **Stay Present**: Throughout the guided meditation, stay present and attentive to the guidance of the instructor. If your mind begins to wander or you become distracted, gently bring your focus back to the sound of the guide's voice or the sensations of your breath. Remember that it's natural for the mind to wander, and each moment of awareness is an opportunity to deepen your practice.

6. **Practice Regularly**: Make guided meditation a regular part of your routine by setting aside time each day or week to practice. Consistency is key to building a meditation habit and experiencing its benefits over time. Start with shorter sessions, such as 5-10 minutes, and gradually increase the duration as you become more comfortable with the practice.

7. **Reflect on Your Experience**: After completing a guided meditation, take a few moments to reflect on your experience. Notice how you feel physically, mentally, and emotionally. Pay attention to any shifts in your mood, energy levels, or perspective. Acknowledge yourself for taking the time to nourish your mind and body through meditation.

By starting simple with guided meditations, you can cultivate a foundation of mindfulness and relaxation that will support you on your meditation journey. As you become more familiar with the practice, you may choose to explore other forms of meditation or develop your own self-guided practice. Remember that meditation is a personal journey, and there's no right or wrong way to practice—just be open, curious, and compassionate with yourself along the way.

Guided meditations are an excellent starting point for beginners who are new to meditation or those looking for additional support in their practice. Guided meditations are led by a teacher or recorded audio that provides instructions and prompts to help you relax, focus your mind, and cultivate mindfulness. Here's how you can start with guided meditations:

1. **Find a Comfortable Space**: Choose a quiet and comfortable space where you can relax without distractions. It could be a quiet room in your home, a peaceful outdoor setting, or any place where you feel safe and at ease.

2. **Select a Guided Meditation**: There are many resources available for guided meditations, including meditation apps, online videos, podcasts, and CDs. Choose a guided meditation that resonates with you and aligns with your intentions for meditation. You may want to explore different styles and teachers to find what works best for you.

3. **Get into a Comfortable Position**: Sit or lie down in a comfortable position that allows you to relax and remain alert. You can sit on a cushion, chair, or yoga mat with your spine straight and your hands resting comfortably in your lap or on your knees. If you prefer, you can also lie down on your back with your arms by your sides and your legs extended comfortably.

4. **Follow the Guidance**: Start the guided meditation and listen to the instructions provided by the teacher or narrator. They may guide you through a series of relaxation techniques, breathing exercises, visualizations, or body scans to help you settle into a state of deep relaxation and presence.

5. **Stay Present and Open**: As you follow along with the guided meditation, try to stay present and open to whatever arises in your experience. Notice any thoughts, emotions, or sensations that come up without judgment, and gently redirect your attention back to the guidance whenever your mind starts to wander.

6. **Practice Regularly**: Consistency is key to developing a meditation practice that feels nourishing and supportive. Aim to practice guided meditation regularly, whether it's once a day, a few times a week, or whenever you feel the need for relaxation and rejuvenation. Over time, you'll become more familiar with the practice and its benefits.

7. **Reflect on Your Experience**: After completing the guided meditation,

take a few moments to reflect on your experience. Notice how you feel physically, mentally, and emotionally. Pay attention to any insights, sensations, or shifts in awareness that may have occurred during the practice.

Starting with guided meditations is an accessible and supportive way to begin your meditation journey. By following the guidance of a skilled teacher or narrator, you can learn valuable techniques for relaxation, mindfulness, and self-awareness that you can carry with you into your daily life.

13

13

Body Scan Meditation

Body scan meditation is a mindfulness practice that involves systematically directing your attention to different parts of your body, cultivating awareness of physical sensations and promoting relaxation. Here's how you can practice body scan meditation:

1. **Find a Comfortable Position**: Begin by finding a comfortable position for meditation, either sitting or lying down. If you're sitting, sit with your back straight and your hands resting comfortably in your lap or on your knees. If you're lying down, lie on your back with your arms by your sides and your legs extended comfortably.

2. **Close Your Eyes**: Close your eyes gently to reduce visual distractions and encourage inward focus.

3. **Take a Few Deep Breaths**: Take a few deep breaths to settle into your body and relax your mind. Inhale deeply through your nose, allowing your abdomen to rise as you fill your lungs with air. Exhale slowly and completely through your mouth, releasing any tension or stress with each breath.

4. **Bring Awareness to Your Body**: Begin by bringing your awareness to your body as a whole, noticing any sensations, tensions, or areas of comfort or discomfort. Take a few moments to simply observe and connect with the present moment.

5. **Start at the Top of Your Head**: Begin the body scan by directing your attention to the top of your head. Notice any sensations, warmth, tingling, or pressure in this area. Allow your awareness to rest on the sensations without trying to change or control them.

6. **Move Down Through Your Body**: Slowly move your attention down through your body, scanning each part from the top of your head to the tips of your toes. Notice any sensations, tensions, or areas of relaxation as you move through each part of your body. You can move systematically from head to toe or choose to focus on specific areas that need attention.

7. **Observe Without Judgment**: As you scan your body, practice observing without judgment or attachment to the sensations you encounter. If you notice areas of tension or discomfort, simply observe them with curiosity and compassion, allowing them to soften and release with each breath.

8. **Stay Present and Gentle**: If your mind begins to wander or you become distracted, gently guide your attention back to the present moment and the sensations in your body. Each time you notice your mind wandering, gently bring it back without judgment or frustration.

9. **End with Full Body Awareness**: Once you've completed the body scan, take a few moments to bring your awareness back to your body as a whole. Notice how you feel physically, mentally, and emotionally after completing the practice. Take a few deep breaths to seal in the benefits of the meditation.

Body scan meditation can be practiced regularly to promote relaxation, reduce stress, and cultivate greater awareness of your body and mind. With consistent practice, you can develop a deeper connection to yourself and enhance your overall well-being.

Body scan meditation is a mindfulness practice that involves systematically directing your attention to different parts of your body, from head to toe, and observing any sensations or tensions that arise. Here's how you can practice body scan meditation:

1. **Find a Comfortable Position**: Start by finding a comfortable position either sitting or lying down. If you choose to lie down, you can do so on your back with your arms by your sides and your legs slightly apart. If you're sitting, sit in a chair or on a cushion with your spine comfortably straight.

2. **Close Your Eyes**: Close your eyes gently and take a few deep breaths to center yourself and relax your body. Allow your breath to flow naturally and effortlessly as you prepare to begin the body scan.

3. **Bring Awareness to Your Breath**: Begin by bringing your awareness to your breath. Notice the sensation of the breath as it enters and leaves your body. Feel the rise and fall of your chest or abdomen with each inhale and exhale.

4. **Start at the Top of Your Head**: Begin the body scan by directing your attention to the top of your head. Notice any sensations, tingling, warmth, or tension in this area. Allow your awareness to rest here for a few moments before moving on.

5. **Move Down Through Your Body**: Slowly and methodically move your attention down through your body, scanning each part from your head to your toes. Notice any sensations or feelings in each area, without trying to change or fix anything. Simply observe what is present with an attitude of curiosity and acceptance.

6. **Observe Sensations**: As you scan each part of your body, pay attention to any sensations that arise, such as warmth, coolness, pressure, tingling, or tightness. Notice the quality and intensity of these sensations without judgment or interpretation.

7. **Release Tension**: If you encounter areas of tension or discomfort during the body scan, you can gently breathe into these areas and imagine them softening and releasing with each exhale. Allow your breath to soothe and relax any areas of tightness or tension.

8. **Complete the Scan**: Continue scanning down through your body, moving slowly and deliberately until you reach your toes. Take a moment to observe your entire body as a whole, noticing any changes or shifts in how you feel.

9. **Return to Your Breath**: Once you've completed the body scan, return your attention to your breath. Notice how your body feels as a whole, and take a few deep breaths to anchor yourself in the present moment.

10. **Reflect on Your Experience**: After completing the body scan, take a few moments to reflect on your experience. Notice how you feel physically, mentally, and emotionally. Acknowledge any insights or observations that arose during the practice.

Body scan meditation is a powerful way to cultivate mindfulness, awareness, and relaxation throughout your entire body. By systematically scanning each part of your body with gentle attention and acceptance, you can cultivate a deeper connection to yourself and promote overall well-being.

14

14

Mindfulness Meditation

Mindfulness meditation is a practice that involves bringing your full attention to the present moment with an attitude of openness, curiosity, and non-judgment. It cultivates awareness of your thoughts, emotions, bodily sensations, and the surrounding environment, allowing you to develop greater clarity, presence, and insight. Here's how you can practice mindfulness meditation:

1. **Find a Quiet Space**: Begin by finding a quiet and comfortable space where you can sit undisturbed for the duration of your meditation. You can sit on a cushion, chair, or yoga mat with your spine comfortably straight and your hands resting on your lap or knees.

2. **Close Your Eyes or Soften Your Gaze**: Close your eyes gently or soften your gaze by lowering your eyelids and resting your gaze on a spot a few feet in front of you. This helps minimize distractions and directs your attention inward.

3. **Bring Awareness to Your Breath**: Start by bringing your awareness to your breath. Notice the sensation of the breath as it enters and leaves your body. Feel the rise and fall of your chest or abdomen with each inhale and exhale. Allow your breath to be natural and effortless, without trying to control it.

4. **Anchor Your Attention**: Use your breath as an anchor to keep your

attention grounded in the present moment. Whenever your mind begins to wander or become distracted by thoughts, gently bring your focus back to your breath. You can do this by silently noting "inhale" as you breathe in and "exhale" as you breathe out.

5. **Notice Thoughts and Emotions**: As you continue to focus on your breath, you may notice thoughts, emotions, or sensations arising in your mind and body. Instead of getting caught up in these thoughts or trying to suppress them, simply observe them with an attitude of curiosity and non-judgment. Notice their transient nature as they come and go, like clouds passing through the sky.

6. **Expand Your Awareness**: As you become more comfortable with the practice, you can expand your awareness to include other aspects of your experience, such as bodily sensations, sounds, or the environment around you. Notice the sensations of the body, the sounds in the room, and the quality of light filtering through your closed eyelids.

7. **Cultivate Acceptance and Compassion**: Throughout your meditation, cultivate an attitude of acceptance and compassion towards yourself and whatever arises in your experience. Embrace all aspects of your present moment experience, whether pleasant or unpleasant, with kindness and understanding.

8. **Practice Non-Attachment**: Remember that the goal of mindfulness meditation is not to eliminate thoughts or emotions, but rather to observe them with equanimity and non-attachment. Allow whatever arises in your awareness to be present without clinging to it or pushing it away.

9. **End with Gratitude**: After your meditation, take a moment to express gratitude for the opportunity to practice mindfulness and cultivate awareness. Notice how you feel physically, mentally, and emotionally after the practice, and carry this sense of presence and clarity with you into the rest of your day.

Mindfulness meditation is a simple yet profound practice that can be integrated into your daily life to cultivate greater awareness, presence, and well-being. By bringing your attention to the present moment with openness and curiosity, you can develop a deeper connection to yourself and the world around you.

Mindfulness meditation is a practice that involves cultivating present-moment awareness and non-judgmental attention to your thoughts, emotions, sensations, and surroundings. Rooted in ancient Buddhist traditions, mindfulness meditation has become increasingly popular in modern times as a way to reduce stress, enhance well-being, and cultivate inner peace. Here's how you can practice mindfulness meditation:

1. **Find a Quiet Space**: Begin by finding a quiet and comfortable space where you can sit undisturbed for the duration of your meditation practice. You can sit on a cushion, chair, or yoga mat, whichever is most comfortable for you.

2. **Assume a Comfortable Posture**: Sit with your spine comfortably straight and your hands resting gently in your lap or on your knees. Close your eyes or keep them softly focused on a spot in front of you.

3. **Bring Attention to Your Breath**: Start by bringing your attention to your breath. Notice the sensation of your breath as it enters and leaves your body. You can focus on the rise and fall of your chest, the feeling of air passing through your nostrils, or the expansion and contraction of your abdomen.

4. **Observe Thoughts and Sensations**: As you continue to focus on your breath, you may notice thoughts, emotions, or sensations arising in your mind and body. Instead of trying to suppress or control these experiences, simply observe them with curiosity and non-judgmental awareness.

5. **Return to the Present Moment**: Whenever you become aware that your mind has wandered away from your breath and into thoughts, gently and without judgment bring your attention back to the present moment and the sensations of your breath. This process of returning to the breath trains your mind to become more focused and present.

6. **Practice Acceptance**: Throughout your meditation practice, practice

accepting whatever arises in your experience without resistance or attachment. Whether it's a feeling of calm or restlessness, joy or sadness, simply acknowledge it with openness and compassion.

7. **Cultivate Kindness and Compassion**: As you continue to practice mindfulness meditation, you may notice patterns of self-criticism or judgment arising in your mind. Cultivate kindness and compassion towards yourself, recognizing that mindfulness is about accepting yourself and your experience just as you are.

8. **Extend Mindfulness to Daily Life**: Beyond your formal meditation practice, seek to cultivate mindfulness in your daily life by bringing present-moment awareness to everyday activities such as eating, walking, or interacting with others. Notice the sights, sounds, smells, and sensations of each moment with curiosity and appreciation.

9. **Practice Regularly**: Like any skill, mindfulness meditation requires regular practice to cultivate. Aim to set aside time each day for formal meditation practice, starting with just a few minutes and gradually increasing the duration as you become more comfortable.

10. **Be Patient and Persistent**: Remember that mindfulness meditation is a journey, and progress often comes gradually over time. Be patient with yourself and trust in the process of mindfulness to unfold naturally as you continue to practice with dedication and persistence.

By cultivating present-moment awareness and non-judgmental acceptance through mindfulness meditation, you can develop a deeper connection to yourself and the world around you, leading to greater peace, clarity, and well-being in your life.

15

15

Loving-Kindness Meditation

Loving-kindness meditation, also known as Metta meditation, is a practice that involves cultivating feelings of love, compassion, and goodwill towards oneself and others. Originating from Buddhist traditions, loving-kindness meditation is a powerful way to cultivate empathy, reduce negative emotions, and foster a sense of connection and well-being. Here's how you can practice loving-kindness meditation:

1. **Find a Comfortable Position**: Begin by finding a comfortable seated position on a cushion, chair, or yoga mat. Close your eyes or keep them softly focused on a spot in front of you.
2. **Cultivate a Loving Attitude Towards Yourself**: Start by directing loving-kindness towards yourself. Repeat silently or aloud phrases that evoke feelings of love, compassion, and well-being towards yourself. Some common phrases you can use include:
3. May I be happy.
4. May I be healthy.
5. May I be safe.
6. May I live with ease.
7. **Extend Loving-Kindness to Others**: After cultivating feelings of loving-kindness towards yourself, gradually extend these feelings towards others. You can start with someone you love deeply, such as a

family member or close friend, and repeat the same phrases of loving-kindness towards them:

8. May [name] be happy.
9. May [name] be healthy.
10. May [name] be safe.
11. May [name] live with ease.
12. **Include Neutral People**: Next, extend loving-kindness towards neutral people, such as acquaintances or strangers. Repeat the phrases of loving-kindness towards them as well:
13. May all beings be happy.
14. May all beings be healthy.
15. May all beings be safe.
16. May all beings live with ease.
17. **Extend Loving-Kindness to Difficult People**: Finally, challenge yourself to extend loving-kindness towards difficult people or those with whom you have conflicts or negative feelings. Repeat the phrases of loving-kindness towards them as a way of cultivating empathy and forgiveness:
18. May [name] find happiness and peace.
19. May [name] be free from suffering.
20. May [name] be filled with love and compassion.
21. May [name] experience inner peace and well-being.
22. **Cultivate an Open Heart**: Throughout the loving-kindness meditation practice, focus on cultivating an open heart and a sense of connection with all beings. Allow yourself to feel the warmth and expansiveness of loving-kindness radiating from your heart towards yourself and others.
23. **Practice Regularly**: Aim to practice loving-kindness meditation regularly, starting with just a few minutes each day and gradually increasing the duration as you become more comfortable. Over time, you'll notice the positive effects of loving-kindness meditation on your mood, relationships, and overall sense of well-being.

By practicing loving-kindness meditation, you can cultivate a deep sense of compassion, empathy, and connection towards yourself and others, fostering greater happiness, harmony, and peace in your life and in the world around you.

Loving-kindness meditation, also known as Metta meditation, is a practice that involves cultivating feelings of love, compassion, and goodwill towards oneself and others. Rooted in Buddhist traditions, loving-kindness meditation is a powerful tool for fostering emotional well-being, empathy, and connection with others. Here's how you can practice loving-kindness meditation:

1. **Find a Quiet Space**: Begin by finding a quiet and comfortable space where you can sit undisturbed for the duration of your meditation practice. Sit on a cushion, chair, or yoga mat in a posture that feels comfortable and supportive.

2. **Set Your Intention**: Start by setting your intention for the practice. This could be a simple statement such as "May I be happy, may I be healthy, may I be safe, may I live with ease." You can also choose to dedicate your practice to someone else, such as a loved one, a friend, or even someone you're having difficulty with.

3. **Focus on Your Breath**: Close your eyes and take a few deep breaths to center yourself and relax your body. Bring your attention to your breath, noticing the sensation of the breath as it enters and leaves your body. Allow your breath to become smooth, steady, and natural.

4. **Cultivate Loving-Kindness Towards Yourself**: Begin by directing loving-kindness towards yourself. Repeat your chosen intention silently in your mind, allowing the words to resonate deeply within you. Visualize yourself surrounded by a warm and loving light, feeling a sense of kindness and compassion towards yourself.

5. **Extend Loving-Kindness to Others**: Once you have cultivated feelings of loving-kindness towards yourself, begin to extend these feelings towards others. Picture someone you love dearly, such as a family member, friend, or mentor, and repeat your intention for their well-being. Imagine sending them waves of love, compassion, and goodwill

from your heart to theirs.

6. **Expand Your Circle of Compassion**: Gradually expand your circle of compassion to include others in your life, such as acquaintances, coworkers, and even strangers. Repeat your intention for their happiness, health, safety, and ease, wishing them well with an open and generous heart.

7. **Include Difficult People**: As you continue your loving-kindness meditation, consider including difficult people or those with whom you may have conflicts or disagreements. Practice extending loving-kindness towards them, recognizing their humanity and inherent worth, and wishing them peace and happiness.

8. **Cultivate Universal Loving-Kindness**: Finally, expand your loving-kindness meditation to include all beings everywhere, without exception. Visualize the entire world bathed in a radiant light of love and compassion, and repeat your intention for the happiness and well-being of all sentient beings.

9. **Return to Your Breath**: Once you have completed your loving-kindness meditation, take a few moments to return to your breath and center yourself in the present moment. Notice how you feel physically, emotionally, and mentally after practicing loving-kindness meditation.

10. **Practice Regularly**: Make loving-kindness meditation a regular part of your mindfulness practice, setting aside time each day to cultivate feelings of love, compassion, and goodwill towards yourself and others. With consistent practice, you can develop greater empathy, connection, and emotional resilience in your life.

By practicing loving-kindness meditation, you can cultivate a heart that is open, generous, and compassionate, fostering greater well-being and harmony within yourself and the world around you.

16

16

Focused Attention Meditation

Focused attention meditation is a mindfulness practice that involves directing and sustaining your attention on a single point of focus, such as your breath, a mantra, or a visual object. This practice helps cultivate concentration, mental clarity, and present-moment awareness. Here's how you can practice focused attention meditation:

1. **Find a Quiet Space**: Begin by finding a quiet and comfortable space where you can sit undisturbed for the duration of your meditation practice. Sit on a cushion, chair, or yoga mat in a posture that feels comfortable and alert.

2. **Choose Your Point of Focus**: Select a single point of focus for your meditation practice. This could be your breath, a specific word or phrase (mantra), a visual object (such as a candle flame or an image), or a sensation in your body (such as the feeling of your feet on the ground).

3. **Settle into Your Posture**: Close your eyes or keep them softly focused on your chosen point of focus. Take a few deep breaths to center yourself and relax your body. Sit with a tall spine and relaxed shoulders, allowing your hands to rest comfortably in your lap or on your knees.

4. **Bring Attention to Your Point of Focus**: Direct your attention to your chosen point of focus. If you've chosen your breath, notice the sensation

of the breath as it enters and leaves your body. If you've chosen a mantra, silently repeat the word or phrase in your mind with each inhale and exhale. If you've chosen a visual object, gaze softly at it with relaxed eyes.

5. **Maintain Your Focus**: As you continue to focus on your chosen point of focus, you may notice thoughts, emotions, or sensations arising in your mind and body. Whenever you become aware that your mind has wandered away from your point of focus, gently and without judgment bring your attention back to it.

6. **Cultivate Concentration**: Practice sustaining your attention on your chosen point of focus for as long as you can without becoming distracted. If your mind wanders, simply acknowledge it with kindness and gently return your attention to your point of focus. Over time, you'll strengthen your ability to concentrate and maintain focus for longer periods.

7. **Observe with Curiosity**: As you continue your focused attention meditation, observe the qualities and nuances of your chosen point of focus with curiosity and openness. Notice any subtle changes or sensations that arise, allowing yourself to experience each moment fully.

8. **Practice Acceptance**: Throughout your meditation practice, practice accepting whatever arises in your experience without resistance or attachment. Whether it's a feeling of calm or restlessness, joy or sadness, simply acknowledge it with openness and compassion.

9. **Conclude Your Meditation**: When you're ready to conclude your meditation, take a few deep breaths and gently transition back to your everyday awareness. Notice how you feel physically, mentally, and emotionally after practicing focused attention meditation.

10. **Reflect on Your Experience**: After completing your meditation practice, take a few moments to reflect on your experience. Notice any changes in your state of mind, level of concentration, or overall sense of well-being. Acknowledge yourself for dedicating time to cultivate focus and mindfulness in your life.

By practicing focused attention meditation regularly, you can develop greater concentration, mental clarity, and present-moment awareness, leading to enhanced overall well-being and inner peace.

Focused attention meditation is a practice that involves directing your attention to a single point of focus, such as your breath, a mantra, or an object, and maintaining your awareness on that point without getting distracted. This practice helps to cultivate concentration, mindfulness, and mental clarity. Here's how you can practice focused attention meditation:

1. **Choose Your Point of Focus**: Start by choosing a point of focus for your meditation practice. This could be your breath, a specific part of your body, a mantra or word, a visual object, or even a sound. Choose something that feels comfortable and accessible to you.

2. **Find a Quiet Space**: Find a quiet and comfortable space where you can sit without distractions. Sit on a cushion, chair, or yoga mat with your spine comfortably straight and your hands resting gently in your lap or on your knees.

3. **Close Your Eyes or Soften Your Gaze**: Close your eyes gently if you feel comfortable doing so, or soften your gaze by focusing on a spot in front of you. Allow your eyelids to become heavy and relaxed as you bring your attention inward.

4. **Focus on Your Point of Focus**: Begin by bringing your attention to your chosen point of focus. For example, if you're focusing on your breath, bring your awareness to the sensation of the breath as it enters and leaves your body. If you're using a mantra, repeat the word silently in your mind with each inhale and exhale.

5. **Notice When Your Mind Wanders**: As you practice focused attention meditation, you may notice that your mind starts to wander or become distracted by thoughts, emotions, or sensations. This is completely normal and to be expected. When you notice your mind wandering, gently and without judgment bring your attention back to your point of focus.

6. **Cultivate Non-Judgmental Awareness**: As you continue to practice, cultivate a sense of non-judgmental awareness towards your thoughts

and distractions. Instead of getting frustrated or discouraged by distractions, simply observe them with curiosity and acceptance, and gently guide your attention back to your point of focus.

7. **Return to Your Point of Focus**: Each time you bring your attention back to your point of focus, anchor yourself in the present moment and re-establish your connection with your chosen object. Notice the sensations, qualities, or qualities of your point of focus with fresh eyes and an open mind.

8. **Practice Persistence and Patience**: Focused attention meditation is a skill that requires practice, patience, and persistence. Be patient with yourself as you cultivate your ability to sustain your attention and concentration over time. With consistent practice, you'll find that your ability to focus improves and distractions become less disruptive.

9. **Extend Your Practice**: As you become more comfortable with focused attention meditation, you can gradually extend the duration of your practice. Start with just a few minutes and gradually increase the length of your sessions as you feel ready. Experiment with different points of focus to keep your practice fresh and engaging.

10. **Reflect on Your Experience**: After completing your meditation session, take a few moments to reflect on your experience. Notice how you feel physically, mentally, and emotionally. Acknowledge any insights or observations that arose during your practice, and carry these insights with you into your daily life.

By practicing focused attention meditation regularly, you can develop greater concentration, mindfulness, and mental clarity, leading to increased inner peace and well-being in your life.

17

17

Walking Meditation

Walking meditation is a mindfulness practice that involves bringing your attention to the present moment as you walk, focusing on the sensations of movement in your body and the environment around you. It offers a way to cultivate mindfulness, relaxation, and presence while integrating meditation into your daily activities. Here's how you can practice walking meditation:

1. **Choose Your Path**: Find a quiet and relatively safe place where you can walk without distractions. This could be a garden, park, beach, or simply a quiet area in your neighborhood. Choose a path that allows you to walk back and forth in a straight line or in a circle.
2. **Stand Tall**: Stand tall with your feet hip-width apart and your arms relaxed by your sides. Take a few moments to center yourself and establish a sense of balance and stability.
3. **Set Your Intention**: Before you begin walking, set your intention for the practice. You might intend to cultivate mindfulness, relaxation, gratitude, or simply to enjoy the experience of walking.
4. **Begin Walking**: Start walking slowly and deliberately, paying close attention to each step you take. Notice the sensations of your feet touching the ground, the shifting of your weight from one foot to the other, and the movement of your legs and hips.

5. **Focus on Your Breath**: Bring your attention to your breath as you walk, syncing your breath with your steps. You might inhale for a certain number of steps and exhale for the same number of steps, or simply breathe naturally and rhythmically as you walk.

6. **Be Present**: Stay present with each moment of walking, observing the sights, sounds, and sensations around you without judgment or analysis. Notice the feeling of the air on your skin, the sounds of nature or city life, and any thoughts or emotions that arise as you walk.

7. **Cultivate Awareness**: As you continue walking, cultivate awareness of your body and mind. Notice any tension or discomfort in your body and see if you can relax and release it with each step. Observe the thoughts and emotions that arise in your mind, allowing them to come and go without getting caught up in them.

8. **Maintain a Gentle Pace**: Walk at a pace that feels comfortable and sustainable for you. You don't need to rush or force anything. Instead, allow your movements to be slow, deliberate, and mindful, savoring each step as it unfolds.

9. **Turn Around Mindfully**: If you're walking back and forth in a straight line, practice turning around mindfully at the end of your path. Pause for a moment before turning, bringing your attention to your breath and the sensations in your body. Then, turn around slowly and deliberately, continuing to walk with awareness.

10. **End Mindfully**: When you're ready to end your walking meditation, bring your attention back to your intention for the practice. Take a few moments to stand still and reflect on your experience, acknowledging any insights or shifts in awareness that may have occurred. Then, slowly transition back to your everyday activities with a sense of gratitude and presence.

Walking meditation offers a simple yet profound way to integrate mindfulness into your daily life, allowing you to experience greater peace, clarity, and connection with yourself and the world around you. Practice regularly and experiment with different environments and intentions to discover what works best for you.

Walking meditation is a mindfulness practice that involves bringing awareness to the act of walking, allowing you to cultivate presence, relaxation, and mindfulness while moving. This practice can be done indoors or outdoors and offers an opportunity to connect with your body and surroundings in a deeper way. Here's how you can practice walking meditation:

1. **Find a Suitable Location**: Choose a quiet and safe place where you can walk without distractions. This could be a park, garden, or any outdoor space with a clear path. If you prefer, you can also practice walking meditation indoors in a spacious room or hallway.

2. **Stand Mindfully**: Begin by standing still for a few moments with your feet hip-width apart and your arms relaxed by your sides. Close your eyes or keep them softly focused on the ground in front of you. Take a few deep breaths to center yourself and prepare for the practice.

3. **Set Your Intention**: Before you start walking, set your intention for the practice. This could be a simple statement such as "I walk in mindfulness" or "I cultivate presence with each step." Let this intention guide your movements and attitude throughout the practice.

4. **Begin Walking Slowly**: Start walking slowly and deliberately, paying attention to each movement of your feet and legs. Notice the sensation of your feet making contact with the ground, the shifting of your weight from one foot to the other, and the rhythm of your steps.

5. **Focus on Your Breath**: Bring your awareness to your breath as you walk, synchronizing your breath with your steps if it feels natural. You can match your inhale with one step and your exhale with the next, or simply maintain a steady and relaxed breathing pattern as you walk.

6. **Observe Your Surroundings**: As you continue walking, bring your attention to your surroundings. Notice the sights, sounds, smells, and sensations around you without getting caught up in them. Allow your awareness to expand to include the entire present moment as you walk.

7. **Stay Present with Your Body**: Throughout the practice, stay connected to your body and the sensations of walking. Notice the movement of

your muscles, the sensations in your feet and legs, and any other physical sensations that arise as you walk. Use your body as an anchor for your awareness in the present moment.

8. **Cultivate Non-Judgmental Awareness**: As with other mindfulness practices, cultivate a sense of non-judgmental awareness towards your experience as you walk. Notice any thoughts, emotions, or distractions that arise without getting carried away by them. Simply observe them with curiosity and acceptance, and gently guide your attention back to the act of walking.

9. **Maintain a Gentle Pace**: As you walk, maintain a gentle and relaxed pace that feels comfortable for you. There's no need to rush or hurry; instead, focus on moving with ease and grace, allowing each step to unfold naturally and mindfully.

10. **End Mindfully**: When you're ready to end your walking meditation, come to a stop and take a few moments to stand still and notice how you feel. Reflect on your experience and acknowledge any insights or observations that arose during the practice. Carry this sense of mindfulness and presence with you as you transition back to your daily activities.

Walking meditation offers a unique opportunity to integrate mindfulness into your everyday life, allowing you to cultivate presence, relaxation, and awareness as you move through the world. By practicing walking meditation regularly, you can deepen your connection to your body, surroundings, and the present moment, leading to greater peace and well-being in your life.

18

18

Developing Consistency in Meditation Practice

onsistency is key to reaping the full benefits of meditation. Establishing a regular practice can help you cultivate mindfulness, reduce stress, and enhance your overall well-being. Here are some strategies for developing consistency in your meditation practice:

1. **Set Realistic Goals**: Start by setting realistic and achievable goals for your meditation practice. Instead of aiming for long sessions right away, begin with shorter sessions, such as 5 or 10 minutes per day, and gradually increase the duration as you become more comfortable.

2. **Schedule Regular Practice Times**: Choose specific times each day to meditate and incorporate them into your daily routine. Whether it's first thing in the morning, during a lunch break, or before bed, having a consistent schedule helps make meditation a habit.

3. **Create a Dedicated Space**: Designate a quiet and comfortable space for your meditation practice where you won't be disturbed. It could be a corner of a room, a cushion or chair in a peaceful area, or even a spot outdoors if weather permits. Having a dedicated space can help signal to your brain that it's time to meditate.

4. **Use Reminders**: Set reminders or alarms on your phone or calendar

to prompt you to meditate at your chosen times. These reminders can help you stay on track and make meditation a priority in your daily life.

5. **Start Small**: If you're struggling to find time for meditation, start with just a few minutes per day. Even a short meditation session can be beneficial, and you can gradually increase the duration as you build consistency.

6. **Find Accountability Partners**: Partnering with a friend, family member, or meditation group can provide accountability and support for your practice. Share your goals with others and check in regularly to discuss your progress and challenges.

7. **Practice Mindful Integration**: Look for opportunities to integrate mindfulness into your daily activities, such as mindful breathing while waiting in line, mindful eating during meals, or mindful walking during your daily commute. These mini-practices can supplement formal meditation sessions and help reinforce mindfulness throughout your day.

8. **Be Flexible**: Life can be unpredictable, and there may be days when it's challenging to stick to your meditation schedule. Be kind to yourself and remain flexible, adjusting your practice as needed to accommodate changes in your routine or circumstances.

9. **Celebrate Progress**: Celebrate your successes and milestones along the way, no matter how small. Recognize the effort and commitment you're putting into your meditation practice and acknowledge the positive changes you're experiencing as a result.

10. **Reflect on Benefits**: Regularly reflect on the benefits of your meditation practice and how it's positively impacting your life. Notice any changes in your mood, stress levels, or overall well-being, and use these observations as motivation to continue meditating consistently.

By implementing these strategies and prioritizing consistency in your meditation practice, you can cultivate mindfulness and inner peace that extends into every aspect of your life. Remember that consistency is about progress, not perfection, so be patient with yourself as you build and maintain your meditation routine.

Consistency is key to reaping the full benefits of meditation. Developing a regular meditation practice can help you cultivate mindfulness, reduce stress, and enhance your overall well-being. Here are some tips for developing consistency in your meditation practice:

1. **Set Realistic Goals**: Start by setting realistic and achievable goals for your meditation practice. Instead of aiming for long meditation sessions right away, begin with shorter sessions that you know you can commit to on a regular basis. For example, start with just 5 or 10 minutes a day and gradually increase the duration as you become more comfortable.

2. **Establish a Routine**: Incorporate meditation into your daily routine by choosing a specific time and place to practice each day. Whether it's first thing in the morning, during your lunch break, or before bed, find a time that works for you and stick to it consistently. Creating a dedicated meditation space can also help signal to your brain that it's time to meditate.

3. **Start Small**: If the idea of daily meditation feels overwhelming, start small by committing to just a few days of meditation each week. Consistency is more important than frequency, so focus on building a habit that you can sustain over the long term. Gradually increase the frequency of your practice as it becomes more ingrained in your routine.

4. **Use Reminders**: Set reminders or cues to prompt you to meditate each day. This could be a recurring alarm on your phone, a sticky note on your bathroom mirror, or a reminder in your calendar. Having a visual or auditory cue can help reinforce your commitment to meditation and make it easier to remember to practice.

5. **Find Accountability**: Share your meditation goals with a friend, family member, or meditation buddy who can help hold you accountable. Knowing that someone else is counting on you to meditate can provide an extra incentive to stick to your practice, especially on days when motivation is low.

6. **Be Flexible**: While consistency is important, it's also essential to be

flexible and adaptable with your meditation practice. Life can be unpredictable, and there may be times when you're unable to meditate at your usual time or place. Instead of beating yourself up about missed sessions, simply do your best to meditate whenever and wherever you can.

7. **Track Your Progress**: Keep track of your meditation sessions using a journal, app, or habit tracker. Seeing your progress over time can be motivating and help reinforce your commitment to consistency. Celebrate small victories and milestones along the way, whether it's completing a certain number of consecutive days or reaching a new meditation milestone.

8. **Be Patient and Kind to Yourself**: Developing consistency in meditation takes time and effort, so be patient and kind to yourself along the way. Remember that meditation is a practice, not a performance, and there's no such thing as a "perfect" meditation session. Embrace the ups and downs of your meditation journey with openness and self-compassion.

By implementing these strategies and committing to your meditation practice with consistency and dedication, you can cultivate a habit that supports your well-being and helps you thrive in all areas of your life.

19

19

Overcoming Common Obstacles in Meditation Practice

Meditation can be a transformative practice, but it's not without its challenges. Here are some common obstacles you may encounter in your meditation practice and strategies for overcoming them:

1. **Restlessness and Impatience**: It's natural for the mind to resist stillness, especially in the beginning stages of meditation. Restlessness and impatience can manifest as fidgeting, racing thoughts, or a constant urge to check the time. To overcome this obstacle, practice patience and persistence. Remind yourself that meditation is a skill that takes time to develop, and progress comes with consistent practice. Experiment with different meditation techniques to find what works best for you, and be gentle with yourself as you navigate moments of restlessness.

2. **Difficulty Concentrating**: Maintaining focus can be challenging, especially with the constant distractions of modern life. If you find it difficult to concentrate during meditation, start by focusing on the breath or a specific point of focus, such as a mantra or visual object. When your mind inevitably wanders, gently bring your attention back to your point of focus without judgment. With practice, you'll strengthen

your ability to concentrate and sustain attention over time.

3. **Physical Discomfort**: Physical discomfort, such as stiffness, pain, or numbness, can be a common obstacle in meditation, particularly if you're sitting for an extended period of time. To alleviate physical discomfort, experiment with different meditation postures, such as sitting on a cushion, chair, or yoga mat, and use props like pillows or blankets for support. Take breaks as needed to stretch and adjust your position, and practice self-compassion by listening to your body's signals and honoring your limitations.

4. **Resistance and Avoidance**: Resistance and avoidance are common defense mechanisms that arise when faced with uncomfortable thoughts or emotions during meditation. Instead of confronting these experiences, you may find yourself procrastinating or making excuses to avoid meditation altogether. To overcome resistance and avoidance, practice self-awareness and cultivate a willingness to sit with whatever arises in your meditation practice, even if it's uncomfortable. Remind yourself that growth often occurs outside of your comfort zone, and embrace the opportunity for self-discovery and healing that meditation provides.

5. **Self-Criticism and Judgment**: It's common to experience self-criticism and judgment during meditation, especially if you feel like you're not "doing it right" or not making progress as quickly as you'd like. To counteract self-criticism and judgment, cultivate self-compassion and self-acceptance. Remind yourself that meditation is a practice, not a performance, and there's no such thing as a "perfect" meditation session. Celebrate your efforts and progress, no matter how small, and approach each meditation with an attitude of kindness and curiosity.

6. **Lack of Time**: Many people cite a lack of time as a barrier to establishing a consistent meditation practice. While it's true that our lives are often busy and hectic, it's also possible to carve out small pockets of time for meditation throughout the day. Even just a few minutes of meditation can make a difference in your overall well-being. Prioritize your mental health by scheduling meditation into your daily routine, whether it's first thing in the morning, during your lunch break, or before bed. Remember

that consistency is more important than duration, so focus on building a habit of regular practice, even if it's just for a few minutes at a time.

7. **Comparing Yourself to Others**: In the age of social media, it's easy to fall into the trap of comparing yourself to others, especially when it comes to meditation. You may see images of serene meditators sitting in perfect stillness and wonder why your own practice doesn't look the same. Remember that everyone's meditation journey is unique, and there's no one "right" way to meditate. Focus on your own experience and progress, and let go of the need to measure up to others' standards. Cultivate self-compassion and celebrate your own growth and achievements, no matter how small.

By recognizing and addressing these common obstacles in your meditation practice, you can develop greater resilience, patience, and self-awareness, leading to a more fulfilling and transformative meditation journey. Remember that meditation is a lifelong practice, and each moment of presence and awareness is an opportunity for growth and healing.

While meditation offers numerous benefits, it's common to encounter obstacles along the way. Here are some strategies for overcoming common obstacles in meditation:

1. **Restlessness and Impatience**: If you find yourself feeling restless or impatient during meditation, acknowledge these feelings without judgment. Remind yourself that meditation is a practice and that it's okay to experience ups and downs. Try incorporating movement-based practices like walking meditation or yoga to help channel excess energy and cultivate calmness.

2. **Difficulty Focusing**: Difficulty focusing is a common challenge in meditation, especially for beginners. If your mind keeps wandering during meditation, gently bring your attention back to your point of focus (e.g., your breath or a mantra) whenever you notice distraction. Use guided meditations or meditation apps to provide structure and guidance for your practice.

3. **Physical Discomfort**: Physical discomfort, such as stiffness or pain, can make it challenging to meditate comfortably. Experiment with different sitting positions, cushions, or chairs to find a posture that works for you. Incorporate gentle stretching or yoga poses before meditation to release tension and promote relaxation in your body.

4. **Sleepiness or Drowsiness**: Feeling sleepy or drowsy during meditation is natural, especially if you're meditating at the end of a long day or early in the morning. Try meditating at a different time of day when you're more alert and awake. Engage your senses by focusing on the sensations of your breath or the sounds in your environment to help stay alert during meditation.

5. **Resistance or Avoidance**: Sometimes, resistance or avoidance can arise when we encounter uncomfortable thoughts or emotions during meditation. Instead of trying to push these feelings away, practice acceptance and allow them to be present without judgment. Remember that discomfort is a natural part of the meditation process and can lead to growth and insight.

6. **Lack of Time**: Many people struggle to find time for meditation amidst busy schedules and competing priorities. Start by setting aside just a few minutes each day for meditation, gradually increasing the duration as you become more comfortable. Look for opportunities to integrate mindfulness into your daily activities, such as mindful eating or walking.

7. **Expectations and Pressure**: Putting pressure on yourself to have a "perfect" meditation session can create unnecessary stress and tension. Let go of expectations and approach meditation with an attitude of openness and curiosity. Remember that every meditation session is different, and there's no right or wrong way to practice.

8. **Self-Criticism and Judgement**: It's common to criticize yourself for not meditating "well enough" or for experiencing difficulties in your practice. Cultivate self-compassion and kindness towards yourself, acknowledging that meditation is a journey with its ups and downs. Treat yourself with the same care and understanding that you would offer to a friend facing similar challenges.

By recognizing and addressing these common obstacles with patience, compassion, and perseverance, you can cultivate a more fulfilling and sustainable meditation practice that supports your overall well-being and growth.

20

20

Dealing with Distractions in Meditation

Distractions are a common challenge in meditation, but learning how to deal with them effectively can deepen your practice and enhance your ability to cultivate mindfulness. Here are some strategies for managing distractions during meditation:

1. **Acknowledge and Accept**: When distractions arise during meditation, acknowledge them without judgment or frustration. Recognize that distractions are a natural part of the human mind and that it's okay to experience them. Instead of resisting or trying to suppress distractions, practice accepting them with an attitude of openness and curiosity.

2. **Refocus Your Attention**: When you notice your mind wandering or getting caught up in distractions, gently refocus your attention on your chosen point of focus, such as your breath, a mantra, or a sensation in your body. Use this anchor to guide your awareness back to the present moment whenever you become aware of distraction.

3. **Label and Let Go**: Another helpful strategy is to label distractions as they arise and then let them go. For example, if you notice your mind wandering to thoughts about work, you can silently label this distraction as "thinking" and then gently return your focus to your breath. This simple act of labeling can create a sense of space between you and your distractions, making it easier to let them pass.

4. **Use the Breath as an Anchor**: The breath is a powerful anchor for attention in meditation. Whenever you find yourself getting distracted, bring your awareness back to the sensation of your breath moving in and out of your body. Focus on the rise and fall of your chest or the feeling of air passing through your nostrils, allowing the breath to ground you in the present moment.

5. **Practice Non-Attachment**: In meditation, it's important to cultivate a sense of non-attachment to distractions. Instead of getting caught up in the content of your thoughts or emotions, observe them with detachment and let them pass without getting entangled in them. Remember that you are not your thoughts, and that distractions have no power unless you give them attention.

6. **Explore the Distraction**: Sometimes, distractions can offer valuable insights into your inner world. Instead of dismissing distractions outright, take a moment to explore them with curiosity and compassion. Notice what triggered the distraction and any underlying emotions or patterns that may be present. This awareness can deepen your understanding of yourself and your meditation practice.

7. **Practice Gentle Persistence**: Dealing with distractions in meditation requires gentle persistence and patience. Whenever you find yourself getting distracted, gently bring your attention back to your point of focus as many times as necessary. Trust that with practice, your ability to stay focused and present will improve over time.

8. **Be Kind to Yourself**: Finally, be kind and compassionate with yourself as you navigate distractions in meditation. It's normal to experience ups and downs in your practice, and there's no such thing as a "perfect" meditation session. Treat yourself with the same care and understanding that you would offer to a friend facing similar challenges.

By applying these strategies with patience and perseverance, you can learn to navigate distractions with greater ease and cultivate a deeper sense of mindfulness and presence in your meditation practice.

Distractions are a natural part of the meditation process, and learning to navigate them skillfully is essential for developing a consistent and effective practice. Here are some strategies for dealing with distractions in meditation:

1. **Acknowledge and Accept**: The first step in dealing with distractions is to acknowledge and accept them without judgment. Instead of becoming frustrated or discouraged when distractions arise, recognize them as normal and natural occurrences in meditation.

2. **Refocus on Your Point of Focus**: When you notice your mind wandering or becoming distracted, gently and without judgment bring your attention back to your chosen point of focus. This could be your breath, a mantra, a sound, or any other anchor you're using in your practice. Refocusing your attention helps bring you back to the present moment and reduces the impact of distractions.

3. **Labeling Distractions**: Another technique for dealing with distractions is to label them as they arise. For example, if you notice your mind wandering, you might silently label the distraction as "thinking" or "planning." This simple act of labeling can help create distance between you and the distraction, making it easier to let go and return to your point of focus.

4. **Use Distractions as Anchors**: Sometimes, distractions themselves can become anchors for your meditation practice. For example, if you hear a car horn outside, you can use that sound as a point of focus, observing it without getting caught up in thoughts or reactions. By embracing distractions in this way, you can cultivate greater mindfulness and resilience in your practice.

5. **Cultivate Non-Judgmental Awareness**: Practice cultivating non-judgmental awareness towards distractions, thoughts, and emotions as they arise during meditation. Instead of getting caught up in judgment or analysis, simply observe them with curiosity and acceptance, allowing them to come and go without attachment.

6. **Use Guided Meditations**: Guided meditations can be helpful for dealing with distractions, especially for beginners. The guidance provided by a teacher or narrator can help keep your attention focused

and provide support when distractions arise. Many meditation apps and online platforms offer a wide range of guided meditations for different purposes and preferences.

7. **Experiment with Different Techniques**: If you find that distractions persist despite your best efforts, experiment with different meditation techniques to see what works best for you. You might try mindfulness of breath, body scan meditation, loving-kindness meditation, or other practices to find one that resonates with you and helps minimize distractions.

8. **Practice Patience and Persistence**: Dealing with distractions in meditation is a skill that takes time and practice to develop. Be patient with yourself as you navigate this process, and remember that each meditation session is an opportunity for learning and growth. With persistence and dedication, you'll gradually become more adept at managing distractions and deepening your meditation practice.

By incorporating these strategies into your meditation practice, you can learn to navigate distractions with greater ease and cultivate a deeper sense of presence, focus, and mindfulness in your life.

21

21

Embracing Silence in Meditation

Silence plays a crucial role in meditation, providing a space for stillness, introspection, and inner exploration. Embracing silence allows you to connect with yourself on a deeper level and cultivate a sense of inner peace and clarity. Here are some ways to embrace silence in your meditation practice:

1. **Create a Quiet Environment**: Start by finding a quiet and peaceful environment where you can meditate without distractions. Choose a space where you feel comfortable and at ease, whether it's a dedicated meditation room, a corner of your home, or a quiet outdoor spot in nature.

2. **Silence Your External Environment**: Minimize external distractions by turning off or silencing electronic devices, closing windows to block out noise, and letting others in your household know that you'll be meditating. Creating a quiet environment can help you immerse yourself more fully in the silence of your meditation practice.

3. **Let Go of Mental Chatter**: Embracing silence in meditation also involves letting go of mental chatter and inner dialogue. As thoughts arise in your mind, observe them without getting caught up in them, and gently guide your attention back to the present moment. Allow your mind to settle into silence, like a calm lake reflecting the clear sky above.

4. **Focus on the Space Between Thoughts**: Instead of trying to suppress or control your thoughts, focus on the space between them. Notice the gaps of silence that naturally occur between thoughts, and allow yourself to rest in this silent space. Cultivating awareness of the silence within can help quiet the mind and deepen your meditation practice.

5. **Listen to the Sounds of Silence**: In addition to external silence, there is also an internal silence that you can tune into during meditation. Listen to the subtle sounds of silence within you, such as the rhythm of your breath, the beating of your heart, or the stillness of your mind. Allow these internal sounds of silence to become your focal point, guiding you deeper into meditation.

6. **Embrace Stillness and Presence**: Embracing silence in meditation is not just about external quietness but also about cultivating inner stillness and presence. Allow yourself to rest in the spaciousness of silence, feeling a sense of peace and tranquility wash over you. Embrace the present moment exactly as it is, without needing to fill it with words or thoughts.

7. **Practice Mindful Listening**: Incorporate mindful listening into your meditation practice by paying attention to the sounds around you with openness and curiosity. Notice the texture, tone, and quality of each sound as it arises and passes away. By cultivating mindful listening, you can deepen your connection to the present moment and the silence within.

8. **Extend Silence Beyond Meditation**: Finally, consider extending the practice of embracing silence beyond your meditation sessions. Cultivate moments of silence throughout your day, whether it's during a quiet walk in nature, a mindful meal, or a few moments of stillness before bed. Embracing silence in your daily life can help you stay grounded, centered, and connected to yourself and the world around you.

By embracing silence in your meditation practice, you can tap into a profound source of inner wisdom, peace, and clarity. Allow yourself to rest in the silence within, trusting that it has the power to nourish and replenish your mind, body, and spirit.

Silence plays a profound role in meditation, offering space for introspection, inner peace, and deepening awareness. Here are some ways to embrace silence in your meditation practice:

1. **Start with Stillness**: Begin your meditation practice by finding a comfortable seated position and allowing your body to settle into stillness. Close your eyes or soften your gaze, and take a few deep breaths to center yourself in the present moment.

2. **Let Go of External Stimuli**: Release your attachment to external stimuli by turning off or minimizing distractions such as electronic devices, background noise, or other sensory inputs. Create a quiet and serene environment that supports your meditation practice.

3. **Focus on Inner Silence**: Shift your attention inward and cultivate an awareness of inner silence. Notice the gaps between your thoughts, the spaces of stillness between your breaths, and the quiet presence that lies beneath the surface of your mind. Allow yourself to rest in this inner silence, letting go of the need to fill every moment with noise or activity.

4. **Observe Without Judgment**: As you meditate in silence, observe whatever arises in your experience without judgment or interpretation. Notice the thoughts, emotions, sensations, and sounds that come and go, allowing them to pass through your awareness like clouds in the sky. Embrace the silence as a container for all aspects of your inner and outer experience.

5. **Cultivate Presence**: Use the silence of meditation as an opportunity to cultivate presence and mindfulness. Bring your full attention to the present moment, anchoring yourself in the here and now through the sensation of your breath, the feeling of your body, or the awareness of your surroundings. Allow yourself to fully inhabit each moment with a sense of openness and curiosity.

6. **Let Silence Speak**: Allow the silence of meditation to speak to you in its own way. Notice any insights, intuitions, or revelations that arise spontaneously in the stillness of your practice. Embrace these moments

of clarity and understanding as gifts from the silence, trusting in the wisdom that emerges from deep within.

7. **Practice Non-Attachment**: Cultivate a sense of non-attachment to both silence and sound in your meditation practice. Recognize that silence is not the absence of sound, but rather a spaciousness that encompasses all sounds and experiences. Embrace the ebb and flow of silence and sound with equanimity and acceptance.

8. **Carry Silence with You**: As you conclude your meditation practice, carry the sense of silence with you into your daily life. Allow it to infuse your interactions, activities, and experiences with a sense of calm, clarity, and presence. Remember that you can always return to the silence within you, no matter where you are or what you're doing.

By embracing silence in your meditation practice, you can deepen your connection to yourself, cultivate inner peace, and tap into the profound wisdom that lies beyond words. Allow silence to be your guide as you journey inward and discover the depths of your own being.

22

22

The Power of Visualization in Meditation

Visualization is a powerful technique used in meditation to enhance focus, cultivate positive emotions, and manifest desired outcomes. By engaging the mind's eye and imagination, visualization can deepen your meditation practice and bring about profound changes in your inner and outer experience. Here's how you can harness the power of visualization in your meditation practice:

1. **Set an Intention**: Begin your meditation practice by setting a clear intention for your visualization. What do you hope to achieve or experience? Whether it's cultivating a sense of peace, healing, abundance, or creativity, clarify your intention before you begin.

2. **Create a Mental Image**: Once you've set your intention, create a vivid mental image or scene in your mind's eye. Use all of your senses to bring this image to life, imagining colors, shapes, textures, sounds, and even scents associated with your visualization.

3. **Engage Emotionally**: As you visualize, engage emotionally with the scene you've created. Allow yourself to feel the emotions associated with your intention, whether it's joy, gratitude, love, or serenity. The more deeply you connect with the emotions of your visualization, the more powerful its effects will be.

4. **Use Guided Visualization**: Guided visualization can be particularly

helpful for beginners or those who struggle to visualize on their own. Listen to guided meditation recordings or use visualization scripts to lead you through a series of images and scenes designed to support your intentions.

5. **Practice Gratitude**: Visualization is an excellent tool for cultivating gratitude and appreciation. Visualize scenes of abundance, blessings, and moments of joy in your life, allowing yourself to fully experience the feelings of gratitude that arise. Regularly practicing gratitude visualization can help shift your mindset towards positivity and abundance.

6. **Visualize Your Goals**: Visualization is a powerful tool for goal setting and achievement. Visualize yourself accomplishing your goals, whether they're related to personal growth, career success, health, or relationships. See yourself overcoming obstacles, achieving milestones, and manifesting your dreams into reality.

7. **Release Limiting Beliefs**: Visualization can help you identify and release limiting beliefs that may be holding you back. Visualize yourself letting go of self-doubt, fear, and negativity, replacing these beliefs with thoughts of empowerment, confidence, and self-love. See yourself stepping into your full potential with clarity and conviction.

8. **Practice Consistently**: Like any skill, visualization requires regular practice to become more effective. Set aside time each day to engage in visualization meditation, starting with just a few minutes and gradually increasing the duration as you become more comfortable. Consistency is key to unlocking the full potential of visualization in your life.

9. **Trust the Process**: Trust that the images and scenes that arise during visualization are meaningful and significant, even if they don't always make sense at first. Allow yourself to surrender to the process and trust in the wisdom of your subconscious mind to guide you towards your highest good.

10. **Reflect and Integrate**: After completing your visualization practice, take a few moments to reflect on your experience. Notice any insights, emotions, or sensations that arose during the visualization. Integrate these experiences into your awareness and carry them with you as you

move forward in your day.

By incorporating visualization into your meditation practice, you can tap into the power of your imagination to create positive change, enhance your well-being, and manifest your deepest desires. Allow yourself to explore the limitless possibilities of visualization and discover the transformative effects it can have on your mind, body, and spirit.

Visualization is a powerful technique that can enhance your meditation practice by harnessing the creative power of your mind to cultivate specific states of consciousness, promote healing, and manifest positive change. Here's how you can harness the power of visualization in your meditation practice:

1. **Set Your Intention**: Begin your meditation session by setting a clear intention for your visualization practice. Whether it's to cultivate feelings of peace, love, abundance, or healing, clarify your intention and hold it in your mind as you begin.

2. **Create a Mental Image**: Close your eyes and visualize a vivid mental image that corresponds to your intention. It could be a peaceful scene in nature, a symbol of love or abundance, or an image of yourself experiencing healing and wholeness. Allow the image to arise naturally in your mind's eye, and let it unfold with clarity and detail.

3. **Engage Your Senses**: As you visualize, engage all of your senses to make the experience as vivid and immersive as possible. Notice the colors, shapes, and textures of the image. Listen to any sounds that accompany the scene. Feel the sensations of warmth, coolness, or breeze on your skin. Engaging your senses helps anchor you in the present moment and deepen the impact of the visualization.

4. **Embody the Experience**: As you continue to visualize, imagine yourself fully embodying the experience depicted in the mental image. Feel the emotions associated with your intention, whether it's peace, joy, gratitude, or healing. Allow yourself to fully immerse in the experience, surrendering to the feelings and sensations that arise.

5. **Repeat Affirmations**: Alongside your visualization, incorporate affirmations or positive statements that reinforce your intention. Repeat these affirmations silently or aloud, allowing them to sink deeply into your subconscious mind. Affirmations can help reprogram limiting beliefs and amplify the effects of your visualization practice.

6. **Release Attachments**: Practice non-attachment to the outcome of your visualization practice. Trust in the power of your mind to create positive change, but let go of any specific expectations or attachments to how things should unfold. Allow the visualization to unfold naturally and trust that it's already working its magic on a deeper level.

7. **Stay Open and Receptive**: After completing your visualization practice, stay open and receptive to any insights, feelings, or synchronicities that arise in your life. Notice how your thoughts, emotions, and behaviors may shift in alignment with your intention. Be open to receiving the gifts of your visualization practice with gratitude and appreciation.

8. **Practice Regularly**: Like any skill, visualization becomes more potent with regular practice. Set aside time each day to engage in visualization meditation, even if it's just for a few minutes. Consistency is key to harnessing the full power of visualization and manifesting lasting change in your life.

By incorporating visualization into your meditation practice, you can tap into the creative power of your mind to cultivate positive states of being, promote healing, and manifest your deepest desires. Trust in the innate wisdom of your imagination and allow visualization to become a transformative tool on your spiritual journey.

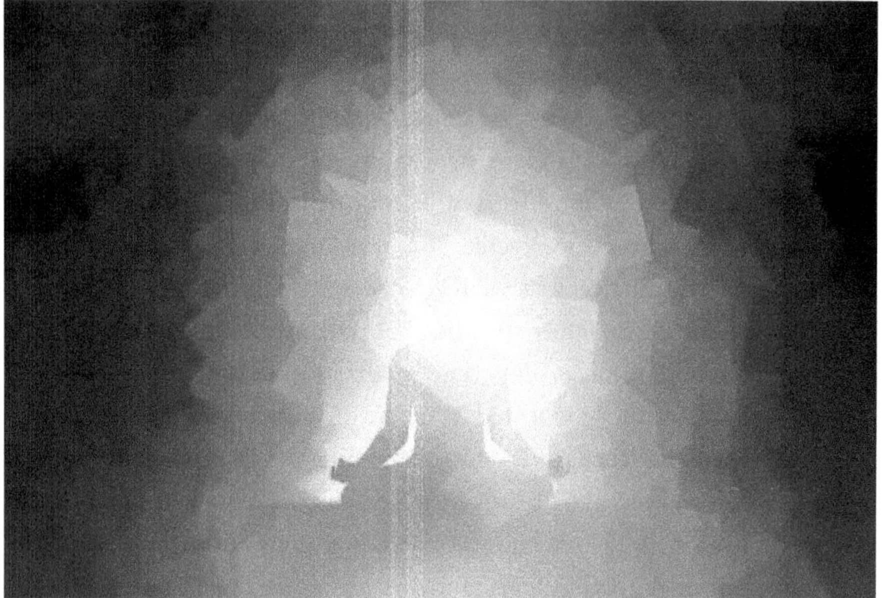

23

23

Transcendental Meditation

Transcendental Meditation (TM) is a widely practiced form of meditation that aims to promote relaxation, reduce stress, and enhance overall well-being. Developed by Maharishi Mahesh Yogi in the 1950s, TM is based on ancient Vedic traditions and involves the use of a mantra—a specific sound or phrase—to focus the mind and induce a state of transcendent awareness. Here's an overview of Transcendental Meditation:

1. **Personalized Mantra**: In TM, practitioners are given a personalized mantra—a specific sound or word—by a trained instructor during a one-on-one session. The mantra is chosen based on various factors, including the individual's age, gender, and temperament. The mantra is used as a focal point during meditation to help quiet the mind and facilitate the experience of transcendent consciousness.

2. **Simple Technique**: TM is known for its simplicity and ease of practice. To meditate, practitioners sit comfortably with their eyes closed and silently repeat their mantra in their mind. Unlike some other forms of meditation that involve concentration or contemplation, TM emphasizes effortlessness, allowing the mind to naturally settle into a state of deep rest and relaxation.

3. **Twenty-Minute Sessions**: TM sessions typically last for about 20 minutes and are practiced twice a day—once in the morning and once

in the evening. The practice can be done sitting comfortably in a chair or cross-legged on the floor, making it accessible to people of all ages and physical abilities.

4. **Effortless Transcendence**: The goal of TM is to transcend ordinary waking consciousness and experience a state of pure awareness or "transcendental consciousness." During meditation, practitioners may experience a sense of deep relaxation, inner peace, and profound stillness. This state of restful alertness is said to have numerous benefits for both mind and body.

5. **Scientific Research**: Transcendental Meditation has been the subject of numerous scientific studies, which have found evidence of its effectiveness in reducing stress, anxiety, and depression, improving cognitive function, and promoting overall well-being. Research suggests that TM may have physiological effects such as reduced blood pressure, improved heart health, and enhanced brain function.

6. **Non-Religious Practice**: TM is a non-religious practice that can be embraced by people of all faiths and backgrounds. While it has its roots in ancient Vedic traditions, TM does not require any specific beliefs or adherence to a particular spiritual tradition. Instead, it is taught as a secular practice focused on promoting health, happiness, and inner peace.

7. **Instruction by Certified Teachers**: Learning TM typically involves attending a series of personalized instruction sessions with a certified TM teacher. During these sessions, the teacher provides guidance on how to practice TM effectively and offers support and encouragement along the way. The personalized nature of the instruction helps ensure that each individual learns the technique correctly and experiences its full benefits.

8. **Global Movement**: Transcendental Meditation has become a global movement, with millions of people around the world practicing the technique. The organization founded by Maharishi Mahesh Yogi, known as the Global Country of World Peace, promotes TM as a tool for creating a more peaceful and harmonious world.

Overall, Transcendental Meditation offers a simple yet powerful approach to meditation that can help individuals reduce stress, enhance well-being, and experience higher states of consciousness. With its emphasis on effortlessness and accessibility, TM has gained popularity as a practical and effective technique for modern-day living.

Transcendental Meditation (TM) is a widely practiced form of silent mantra meditation developed by Maharishi Mahesh Yogi. It is a simple, natural technique that is typically practiced for 15-20 minutes twice a day while sitting comfortably with closed eyes. Here's an overview of Transcendental Meditation:

1. **Mantra-Based Practice**: In Transcendental Meditation, practitioners are given a specific mantra—a word or sound—to repeat silently to themselves. The mantra is chosen by a trained TM teacher based on a person's age and gender and is used as a vehicle to transcend ordinary thinking and access deeper levels of consciousness.

2. **Effortless Technique**: TM is known for its simplicity and ease of practice. Unlike some forms of meditation that require concentration or control of the mind, TM is effortless, allowing the mind to naturally settle into a state of deep relaxation and inner stillness.

3. **Transcending Surface Levels of Consciousness**: The goal of Transcendental Meditation is to transcend the surface levels of waking, dreaming, and sleeping consciousness and experience a state of pure awareness or transcendental consciousness. During TM practice, the mind settles into a state of restful alertness, characterized by a sense of inner peace, clarity, and expanded awareness.

4. **Benefits**: Research has shown that Transcendental Meditation offers a wide range of physical, mental, and emotional benefits. These may include reduced stress and anxiety, improved cognitive function, enhanced creativity, better sleep, and overall greater well-being.

5. **Taught by Certified Teachers**: Transcendental Meditation is typically taught in a series of personal instruction sessions by a certified TM teacher. During these sessions, the teacher provides personalized

instruction on how to practice TM effectively and answers any questions that may arise.

6. **Non-Religious Practice**: TM is a non-religious practice that can be practiced by people of all faiths or belief systems. It does not require any specific beliefs, rituals, or lifestyle changes, making it accessible to people from diverse backgrounds.

7. **Global Movement**: Transcendental Meditation has become a global movement, with millions of people practicing TM worldwide. It has been taught to people of all ages and walks of life, including celebrities, business leaders, athletes, and students.

8. **Research and Scientific Validation**: Over the past several decades, numerous scientific studies have been conducted on Transcendental Meditation, documenting its benefits and effects on various aspects of health and well-being. This research has contributed to the growing recognition and acceptance of TM within the scientific and medical communities.

Overall, Transcendental Meditation offers a simple yet powerful technique for accessing deeper levels of consciousness and experiencing profound states of inner peace and awareness. Whether practiced for stress reduction, personal growth, or spiritual development, TM has the potential to positively impact all areas of life.

24

24

Zen Meditation (Zazen)

Zen meditation, also known as Zazen, is a central practice in Zen Buddhism, emphasizing mindfulness, concentration, and insight. Here's an overview of Zen meditation (Zazen):

1. **Seated Meditation**: Zazen is typically practiced in a seated position on a meditation cushion (zafu) or bench (seiza). The posture is characterized by a stable and upright sitting position, with the spine straight and the hands placed in a specific mudra, such as the cosmic mudra or the Gyan mudra.

2. **Focus on the Breath**: During Zazen, practitioners focus their attention on the breath, using it as an anchor to cultivate mindfulness and concentration. The breath is observed naturally, without trying to control or manipulate it. As thoughts, emotions, or sensations arise, practitioners gently return their attention to the breath, letting go of distractions.

3. **Open Awareness**: In addition to focusing on the breath, Zazen also cultivates open awareness, allowing practitioners to observe the unfolding of experience without attachment or judgment. This open awareness includes being present to whatever arises in the mind and body, whether it's thoughts, feelings, sounds, or sensations.

4. **Non-Dual Awareness**: Zazen aims to cultivate non-dual awareness,

transcending the dualistic distinctions between self and other, subject and object. Through sustained practice, practitioners may experience moments of profound insight or realization, known as Kensho or Satori, in which the illusion of separateness is temporarily dissolved.

5. **Stillness and Silence**: Zazen is characterized by stillness and silence, both externally and internally. Practitioners sit in silence, with minimal movement, allowing the mind to settle and the body to relax. This stillness and silence create a conducive environment for deepening meditation and accessing deeper states of consciousness.

6. **Guidance from a Teacher**: In Zen tradition, guidance from a qualified teacher (Roshi) is considered essential for proper instruction and support in Zazen practice. The teacher provides guidance on posture, technique, and understanding, as well as offering encouragement and insight along the path.

7. **Integration into Daily Life**: Zazen is not limited to formal meditation sessions but is intended to be integrated into all aspects of daily life. Practitioners are encouraged to carry the mindfulness and presence cultivated in Zazen into their everyday activities, whether eating, walking, working, or interacting with others.

8. **Community and Practice Centers**: Zen meditation is often practiced in community settings, such as Zen centers or monasteries, where practitioners come together for group meditation sessions, teachings, and ceremonies. The sense of community and shared practice can provide valuable support and inspiration on the spiritual path.

Overall, Zen meditation (Zazen) offers a simple yet profound practice for cultivating mindfulness, concentration, and insight, leading to greater clarity, peace, and awakening. Through regular practice and dedication, practitioners can deepen their understanding of themselves and the nature of reality, embodying the timeless wisdom of Zen Buddhism.

Zen Meditation, also known as Zazen, is a central practice in Zen Buddhism that emphasizes seated meditation as a means of cultivating mindfulness, insight, and awakening. Here's an overview of Zen Meditation (Zazen):

1. **Seated Meditation**: Zazen is primarily practiced in a seated position on a meditation cushion (zafu) or bench (seiza). The posture is typically upright with a straight spine, relaxed shoulders, and hands placed in a specific mudra position, such as the cosmic mudra or the lotus mudra.

2. **Breath Awareness**: In Zazen, practitioners focus their attention on the breath as it naturally flows in and out of the body. Rather than controlling or manipulating the breath, the emphasis is on simply observing the breath with awareness and equanimity.

3. **Non-Attachment to Thoughts**: During Zazen, thoughts, emotions, and sensations may arise in the mind. Practitioners are encouraged to observe these mental phenomena without attachment or aversion, allowing them to come and go freely without getting caught up in them.

4. **Stillness and Presence**: Zazen cultivates a sense of stillness, presence, and inner peace through the practice of sitting meditation. By grounding themselves in the present moment and letting go of distractions, practitioners can access deeper states of awareness and insight.

5. **Kinhin (Walking Meditation)**: In some Zen traditions, Zazen may be interspersed with periods of walking meditation known as Kinhin. During Kinhin, practitioners walk slowly and mindfully in a circle, synchronizing their movements with their breath and maintaining awareness of each step.

6. **Silent Group Practice**: Zazen is often practiced in silent group settings, known as Zen centers or meditation halls (zendo). Practitioners gather together to sit in meditation, supported by the collective energy of the group and guided by a Zen teacher (sensei) or senior practitioners.

7. **Koan Practice (Optional)**: In certain Zen traditions, practitioners may engage in koan practice as a means of deepening their meditation experience. Koans are paradoxical riddles or questions designed to provoke insight and break through conceptual thinking. Examples include "What is the sound of one hand clapping?" and "What was your original face before you were born?"

8. **Integration into Daily Life**: Zen Meditation is not limited to formal sitting practice but extends into all aspects of daily life. Practitioners are

encouraged to carry the spirit of mindfulness and presence cultivated in Zazen into their everyday activities, whether eating, working, or interacting with others.

9. **Direct Pointing to the Mind**: Zen Meditation is often characterized by its direct and experiential approach to awakening. Rather than relying solely on scriptures or philosophical teachings, Zen emphasizes direct realization of one's true nature or Buddha nature through direct experience and insight.

10. **Open-Handed Awareness**: In Zazen, practitioners cultivate an open-handed awareness that is receptive to whatever arises in the present moment. This non-grasping attitude allows for greater freedom and flexibility of mind, enabling practitioners to respond skillfully to whatever life presents.

Overall, Zen Meditation (Zazen) offers a profound path of self-discovery, awakening, and liberation, inviting practitioners to explore the depths of their own minds and uncover the inherent wisdom and compassion that lies within.

25

25

Kundalini Meditation

Kundalini Meditation is a powerful practice rooted in Kundalini Yoga, a spiritual tradition that aims to awaken and harness the dormant energy (kundalini) believed to reside at the base of the spine. Kundalini Meditation incorporates various techniques, including breathwork, mantra chanting, movement, and visualization, to awaken this energy and facilitate spiritual growth and transformation. Here's an overview of Kundalini Meditation:

1. **Awakening Kundalini Energy**: Kundalini Meditation is designed to awaken and activate the kundalini energy, which is often depicted as a coiled serpent resting at the base of the spine. This energy is believed to represent the divine potential within each individual and is said to rise through the chakras, or energy centers, along the spine when awakened.

2. **Breathwork (Pranayama)**: Breathwork is a central component of Kundalini Meditation. Practitioners use specific breathing techniques, known as pranayama, to regulate and direct the flow of prana, or life force energy, throughout the body. Breathwork helps to balance the nervous system, increase vitality, and prepare the body for deeper meditation.

3. **Mantra Chanting (Japa)**: Mantra chanting is another key aspect of Kundalini Meditation. Practitioners repeat sacred sounds, words, or

phrases, known as mantras, to focus the mind and elevate consciousness. Mantra chanting can help quiet the chatter of the mind, deepen concentration, and connect with higher states of awareness.

4. **Movement and Asana**: Kundalini Meditation may involve gentle movement and yoga asana (postures) to release tension, open energy channels, and prepare the body for meditation. These movements are often fluid and rhythmic, allowing practitioners to embody the flow of energy within the body and cultivate a sense of inner harmony.

5. **Visualization (Yantra and Mudra)**: Visualization techniques, such as yantra (sacred geometric symbols) and mudra (hand gestures), may be used in Kundalini Meditation to focus the mind and channel energy. Practitioners visualize specific images or symbols associated with the awakening of consciousness and spiritual evolution.

6. **Guided Meditation and Meditation Music**: Kundalini Meditation sessions may be guided by a teacher or accompanied by meditation music specifically designed to enhance the meditative experience. Guided meditations provide instruction and support for practitioners, while meditation music creates a conducive atmosphere for relaxation and inner exploration.

7. **Chakra Activation**: Kundalini Meditation often focuses on activating and balancing the seven main chakras, or energy centers, along the spine. Each chakra is associated with specific qualities, such as creativity, intuition, and spiritual awakening. By working with the chakras, practitioners aim to unlock their full potential and experience greater vitality and wholeness.

8. **Spiritual Awakening and Transformation**: The ultimate goal of Kundalini Meditation is spiritual awakening and transformation. As the kundalini energy rises through the chakras, practitioners may experience profound shifts in consciousness, expanded awareness, and a deepening connection to the divine within and without.

Kundalini Meditation is a dynamic and transformative practice that invites practitioners to explore the depths of their being and awaken to their true nature. Through breathwork, mantra chanting, movement, and visualization, individuals can tap into the powerful energy of Kundalini and embark on a journey of self-discovery, healing, and spiritual evolution.

Kundalini Meditation is a powerful practice rooted in Kundalini Yoga, a form of yoga that focuses on awakening the dormant energy (kundalini) that resides at the base of the spine. Kundalini Meditation involves various techniques aimed at activating and harnessing this energy to promote spiritual growth, self-awareness, and transformation. Here's an overview of Kundalini Meditation:

1. **Awakening Kundalini Energy**: The primary aim of Kundalini Meditation is to awaken the dormant Kundalini energy, which is believed to reside at the base of the spine in the subtle energy body. Through specific meditation practices, practitioners seek to awaken this energy and guide it upwards through the energy centers (chakras) along the spine, leading to states of higher consciousness and spiritual awakening.

2. **Breathwork (Pranayama)**: Kundalini Meditation often incorporates various breathwork techniques (pranayama) to awaken and channel the Kundalini energy. Practices such as Breath of Fire (rapid rhythmic breathing), Alternate Nostril Breathing (Nadi Shodhana), and Long Deep Breathing are commonly used to energize the body and balance the flow of energy.

3. **Mantra Meditation**: Mantra repetition is another key component of Kundalini Meditation. Practitioners chant specific mantras, often in Sanskrit, which are believed to have vibrational qualities that resonate with the energy centers (chakras) in the body. Mantras may be repeated silently or aloud to focus the mind, awaken inner awareness, and align with higher states of consciousness.

4. **Visualization (Drishti)**: Visualization techniques are used in Kundalini Meditation to direct and concentrate the flow of Kundalini energy. Practitioners may visualize the energy rising through the central energy channel (sushumna) along the spine or visualize specific imagery associated with each chakra, such as colors, symbols, or geometric

shapes.

5. **Mudras and Bandhas**: Kundalini Meditation often incorporates hand gestures (mudras) and energetic locks (bandhas) to facilitate the flow of energy and enhance the meditative experience. Mudras, such as Gyan Mudra (thumb and index finger touching), are believed to stimulate specific energy pathways, while bandhas, such as Mula Bandha (root lock), help contain and redirect the flow of Kundalini energy.

6. **Guided Meditations and Kriyas**: Kundalini Meditation may involve guided meditations and structured sequences of exercises known as kriyas. These kriyas typically combine breathwork, mantra, movement, and meditation in a specific sequence designed to activate and balance the body's energy centers and facilitate spiritual awakening.

7. **Integration and Self-Reflection**: Kundalini Meditation is not just about the practices themselves but also about integrating the experiences and insights gained during meditation into daily life. Practitioners are encouraged to cultivate self-awareness, self-reflection, and mindfulness in their everyday activities, fostering a deeper connection to the self and the world around them.

8. **Guidance from a Qualified Teacher**: Kundalini Meditation is a profound practice that can have powerful effects on the body, mind, and spirit. It is recommended to seek guidance from a qualified Kundalini Yoga teacher or experienced practitioner who can provide instruction, support, and guidance on the practice, ensuring safety and efficacy.

Overall, Kundalini Meditation offers a transformative path of self-discovery, spiritual growth, and awakening, inviting practitioners to tap into their inner potential and connect with the universal source of energy and consciousness. With dedication, practice, and guidance, Kundalini Meditation can lead to profound states of inner peace, clarity, and realization.

26

26

Chakra Meditation

Chakra Meditation is a spiritual practice that focuses on balancing and activating the seven energy centers, known as chakras, located along the spine. Each chakra is associated with specific qualities, elements, colors, and functions, and Chakra Meditation aims to harmonize these energy centers to promote physical, emotional, and spiritual well-being. Here's an overview of Chakra Meditation:

1. **Understanding the Chakras**: In Chakra Meditation, practitioners work with the seven main chakras, which are located from the base of the spine to the crown of the head. These chakras are:

- Root Chakra (Muladhara)
- Sacral Chakra (Svadhisthana)
- Solar Plexus Chakra (Manipura)
- Heart Chakra (Anahata)
- Throat Chakra (Vishuddha)
- Third Eye Chakra (Ajna)
- Crown Chakra (Sahasrara)

1. **Balancing the Chakras**: The goal of Chakra Meditation is to balance and align the energy flow within each chakra, ensuring that energy

moves freely throughout the body. Imbalances in the chakras can manifest as physical, emotional, or psychological issues, and Chakra Meditation seeks to address these imbalances to promote overall well-being.

2. **Visualization and Breathwork**: Chakra Meditation often involves visualization techniques and specific breathwork exercises to focus awareness on each chakra and facilitate energy flow. Practitioners may visualize each chakra as a spinning wheel of colored light, breathing into and out of each chakra to clear blockages and restore balance.

3. **Mantra and Affirmations**: Mantras and affirmations are commonly used in Chakra Meditation to stimulate and activate the energy centers. Each chakra is associated with a specific seed mantra (bija mantra) and affirmations that resonate with its qualities and attributes. By chanting these mantras or repeating affirmations, practitioners can deepen their connection to each chakra and reinforce positive energy flow.

4. **Mudras and Postures**: Mudras (hand gestures) and specific yoga postures (asanas) may also be incorporated into Chakra Meditation to enhance the energetic effects of the practice. Each chakra is associated with specific mudras and postures that help channel and direct the flow of energy within the body, promoting balance and alignment.

5. **Guided Meditation and Self-Healing**: Guided Chakra Meditations are available in various forms, including audio recordings, videos, and in-person sessions with a meditation teacher or practitioner. These guided meditations typically lead practitioners through a series of visualizations, breathwork exercises, and affirmations designed to balance and activate the chakras and facilitate self-healing on physical, emotional, and spiritual levels.

6. **Integration and Lifestyle Practices**: Chakra Meditation is not limited to formal meditation sessions but extends into daily life through lifestyle practices that support overall well-being. Practitioners are encouraged to cultivate mindfulness, self-awareness, and self-care habits that nurture and sustain the balanced flow of energy within the chakras.

Overall, Chakra Meditation offers a holistic approach to healing and transformation, addressing the interconnectedness of mind, body, and spirit. By working with the chakras through visualization, breathwork, mantra, and mindfulness practices, practitioners can cultivate greater balance, vitality, and harmony in all aspects of their lives.

Chakra Meditation is a practice that focuses on activating, balancing, and harmonizing the body's energy centers, known as chakras. These energy centers are believed to correspond to different aspects of our physical, emotional, and spiritual well-being. Chakra Meditation involves various techniques aimed at clearing blockages and restoring the free flow of energy throughout the body. Here's an overview of Chakra Meditation:

1. **Understanding the Chakras**: Chakras are subtle energy centers located along the central channel of the body, from the base of the spine to the crown of the head. There are seven main chakras, each associated with a specific color, element, sound, and aspect of consciousness. These chakras are:

- Root Chakra (Muladhara)
- Sacral Chakra (Swadhisthana)
- Solar Plexus Chakra (Manipura)
- Heart Chakra (Anahata)
- Throat Chakra (Vishuddha)
- Third Eye Chakra (Ajna)
- Crown Chakra (Sahasrara)

1. **Activating the Chakras**: Chakra Meditation involves techniques to activate and awaken the energy within each chakra. This may include visualization, breathwork, chanting, mantra repetition, and specific yoga poses (asanas) designed to stimulate the flow of energy to each energy center.
2. **Balancing and Harmonizing**: The goal of Chakra Meditation is to balance and harmonize the energy flow within the chakras, ensuring that

no energy center is overactive or underactive. By bringing the chakras into balance, practitioners can experience greater vitality, emotional stability, mental clarity, and spiritual awakening.

3. **Chakra Visualization**: One common technique in Chakra Meditation is to visualize each chakra as a spinning wheel of energy, radiating its characteristic color and qualities. Practitioners may imagine a stream of light or energy flowing into each chakra, clearing away any blockages and restoring its natural balance and vitality.

4. **Breathwork and Pranayama**: Breathwork techniques, such as alternate nostril breathing (Nadi Shodhana) or deep belly breathing, can help activate and cleanse the chakras by regulating the flow of prana (life force energy) throughout the body. By coordinating the breath with specific movements or visualizations, practitioners can facilitate the movement of energy through the chakras.

5. **Chanting and Mantra Meditation**: Chanting specific Sanskrit seed syllables (bija mantras) associated with each chakra can help activate and harmonize the energy within the corresponding energy center. Mantras may be repeated silently or aloud during meditation to invoke the qualities and attributes of each chakra.

6. **Yoga Asanas and Movement**: Certain yoga poses (asanas) can target specific areas of the body associated with each chakra, helping to release tension, stimulate circulation, and activate the corresponding energy centers. Practicing yoga asanas mindfully and with awareness can enhance the benefits of Chakra Meditation.

7. **Self-Reflection and Integration**: Chakra Meditation is not just about activating and balancing the chakras but also about self-reflection, inner exploration, and personal growth. Practitioners are encouraged to observe their thoughts, emotions, and sensations during meditation, cultivating greater self-awareness and understanding.

By incorporating these techniques into their meditation practice, individuals can awaken the latent energy within the chakras, restore balance and harmony to the body-mind-spirit system, and experience greater health, vitality, and well-being on all levels.

27

27

Yoga Nidra

Yoga Nidra, often referred to as "yogic sleep," is a powerful meditation and relaxation practice that induces deep physical, mental, and emotional relaxation while maintaining full awareness and consciousness. Originating from ancient yoga traditions, Yoga Nidra is practiced lying down in a comfortable position, typically at the end of a yoga session or as a standalone practice. Here's an overview of Yoga Nidra:

1. **Deep Relaxation**: The primary aim of Yoga Nidra is to induce a state of deep relaxation in which the body, mind, and spirit can unwind and rejuvenate. Through a guided meditation process, practitioners systematically relax different parts of the body, release tension, and surrender to a state of profound stillness and ease.

2. **Guided Meditation**: Yoga Nidra is typically guided by a teacher or recorded audio, leading practitioners through a series of instructions and visualizations. The guided meditation may involve body scanning, breath awareness, rotation of consciousness, and guided imagery to promote relaxation and inner peace.

3. **Systematic Relaxation**: During Yoga Nidra, practitioners are guided to systematically relax different parts of the body, starting from the toes and working their way up to the crown of the head. By consciously

releasing tension and letting go of muscular effort, practitioners create a sense of physical ease and comfort.

4. **Breath Awareness**: Breath awareness is a key component of Yoga Nidra, helping to anchor the mind in the present moment and regulate the nervous system. Practitioners are encouraged to observe the natural flow of their breath, noticing its rhythm, depth, and quality without trying to control or manipulate it.

5. **Inner Exploration**: Yoga Nidra provides a unique opportunity for inner exploration and self-inquiry. As practitioners relax deeply, they may become more attuned to their thoughts, emotions, sensations, and unconscious patterns. Through gentle observation and non-judgmental awareness, practitioners can cultivate greater self-awareness and insight.

6. **Sankalpa (Intention Setting)**: At the beginning or end of Yoga Nidra, practitioners may set a sankalpa or intention—a positive affirmation or statement of purpose. The sankalpa is repeated silently during the practice, sinking into the subconscious mind and influencing one's thoughts, actions, and choices.

7. **Accessing the Subconscious Mind**: Yoga Nidra is said to provide access to the subconscious mind, where deep-seated patterns, beliefs, and memories reside. By entering a state of deep relaxation and heightened receptivity, practitioners can explore and transform limiting beliefs, heal past traumas, and cultivate positive change at a subconscious level.

8. **Benefits**: Yoga Nidra offers a wide range of benefits for physical, mental, and emotional well-being. These may include stress reduction, improved sleep, enhanced concentration and focus, relief from anxiety and depression, increased creativity, and a greater sense of inner peace and harmony.

Overall, Yoga Nidra is a profound practice that offers a doorway to deep relaxation, self-discovery, and spiritual awakening. By surrendering to the innate wisdom of the body and mind, practitioners can experience profound healing and transformation on all levels of their being.

Yoga Nidra, often referred to as "yogic sleep," is a powerful meditation and relaxation technique that induces a state of deep relaxation while maintaining full consciousness. Originating from ancient yogic traditions, Yoga Nidra is practiced lying down in a comfortable position and is characterized by guided meditation, body scanning, and visualization. Here's an overview of Yoga Nidra:

1. **Guided Relaxation**: Yoga Nidra typically begins with a guided relaxation, where the practitioner is led through a progressive relaxation of the body. Starting from the toes and moving upwards to the crown of the head, each body part is consciously relaxed, releasing tension and promoting a state of physical ease and comfort.

2. **Breath Awareness**: Throughout the practice, practitioners maintain awareness of their breath, observing the natural rhythm of inhalation and exhalation. By focusing on the breath, practitioners anchor themselves in the present moment and cultivate a sense of inner calm and presence.

3. **Body Scanning**: A key component of Yoga Nidra is the systematic body scanning technique, where practitioners bring their attention to different parts of the body sequentially. By mentally scanning each body part, practitioners develop heightened awareness of physical sensations and subtle energy flow, promoting relaxation and inner awareness.

4. **Rotation of Consciousness**: In Yoga Nidra, practitioners may be guided through a rotation of consciousness, where attention is systematically directed to different regions of the body. This process helps cultivate mindfulness and sensory awareness, allowing practitioners to experience deep relaxation and inner stillness.

5. **Visualization and Imagery**: Yoga Nidra often incorporates visualization and imagery techniques to deepen the meditative experience. Practitioners may be guided to visualize calming scenes or symbols, such as a tranquil beach or a peaceful forest, fostering a sense of relaxation and inner peace.

6. **Sankalpa (Intention Setting)**: During Yoga Nidra, practitioners have

the opportunity to set a sankalpa, or a positive affirmation or intention. This intention is repeated silently in the mind, planting the seeds of positive change and transformation at a subconscious level.

7. **Deep Relaxation and Healing**: Through the practice of Yoga Nidra, practitioners enter a state of deep relaxation that is conducive to healing and rejuvenation on all levels—physical, mental, and emotional. The practice allows for the release of accumulated stress, tension, and fatigue, promoting overall well-being and vitality.

8. **Accessible to All**: One of the unique aspects of Yoga Nidra is its accessibility to people of all ages, abilities, and fitness levels. Since the practice is done lying down in a comfortable position, it can be easily adapted to accommodate individual needs and preferences.

Overall, Yoga Nidra offers a profound journey into the realm of deep relaxation, self-discovery, and inner transformation. By integrating this ancient practice into their lives, practitioners can experience profound benefits for their health, well-being, and spiritual growth.

28

28

Mindful Eating

Mindful Eating is a practice that involves bringing full awareness and attention to the experience of eating, with a focus on the sensory aspects of food and the sensations within the body. Rooted in mindfulness meditation principles, Mindful Eating encourages a non-judgmental awareness of food choices, eating habits, and the body's hunger and fullness cues. Here's an overview of Mindful Eating:

1. **Present Moment Awareness**: Mindful Eating emphasizes being fully present and engaged in the eating experience. Rather than eating on autopilot or multitasking, practitioners bring their attention to the present moment, savoring each bite of food with mindful awareness.

2. **Engaging the Senses**: Mindful Eating involves using all five senses—sight, smell, taste, touch, and hearing—to fully experience the colors, aromas, textures, flavors, and sounds of food. By engaging the senses, practitioners deepen their connection to the eating experience and enhance their enjoyment of food.

3. **Non-Judgmental Observation**: Mindful Eating encourages a non-judgmental attitude towards food choices, eating habits, and the body. Rather than labeling foods as "good" or "bad," practitioners observe their thoughts, emotions, and physical sensations without criticism or attachment, fostering a compassionate relationship with food and the

body.

4. **Eating with Awareness**: Mindful Eating involves slowing down the pace of eating and paying attention to the process of chewing, swallowing, and digesting food. Practitioners take the time to savor each bite, noticing the sensations of hunger, fullness, and satisfaction as they arise.

5. **Mindful Meal Preparation**: Mindful Eating extends beyond the act of eating to include the entire food experience, including meal planning, shopping, and preparation. Practitioners approach these activities with mindfulness and intention, making conscious choices that support their health and well-being.

6. **Recognizing Hunger and Fullness**: Mindful Eating encourages tuning into the body's hunger and fullness cues to guide eating behavior. Practitioners learn to distinguish between physical hunger and other types of hunger, such as emotional or environmental cues, and to eat in response to genuine hunger while stopping when satisfied.

7. **Cultivating Gratitude**: Mindful Eating fosters a sense of gratitude for the food we eat and the nourishment it provides. Practitioners acknowledge the interconnectedness of food with the natural world, expressing appreciation for the farmers, producers, and all those involved in bringing food to the table.

8. **Building Awareness of Triggers**: Mindful Eating helps practitioners become more aware of their emotional and environmental triggers for eating, such as stress, boredom, or social influences. By recognizing these triggers, practitioners can develop healthier coping strategies and make conscious choices about when, what, and how much to eat.

Overall, Mindful Eating offers a holistic approach to nourishing the body, mind, and spirit, promoting greater awareness, satisfaction, and well-being in relation to food and eating. By cultivating mindfulness in eating, practitioners can develop a more balanced and harmonious relationship with food, leading to improved health, vitality, and happiness.

Mindful Eating is a practice that involves bringing full awareness and attention to the process of eating, savoring each bite, and being fully present in the moment. It draws upon principles of mindfulness, encouraging individuals to cultivate a deeper connection with their food, body, and overall eating experience. Here's an overview of Mindful Eating:

1. **Present Moment Awareness**: Mindful Eating involves bringing attention to the present moment without judgment. Practitioners focus on the sensory experience of eating—sight, smell, taste, texture, and even sound—while letting go of distractions and preoccupations.

2. **Engaging the Senses**: When practicing Mindful Eating, individuals engage all their senses to fully experience the food they are eating. They observe the colors, shapes, and textures of the food, inhale its aroma, notice the flavors on their palate, and feel the sensations of chewing and swallowing.

3. **Slowing Down**: Mindful Eating encourages individuals to eat slowly and with intention, taking the time to savor each bite and fully experience the process of eating. By slowing down, practitioners can tune into their body's hunger and fullness cues, leading to greater satisfaction and enjoyment of food.

4. **Non-Judgmental Awareness**: Practitioners approach the eating experience with non-judgmental awareness, accepting their thoughts, feelings, and sensations without criticism or self-criticism. They cultivate a sense of curiosity and openness towards their eating habits, preferences, and attitudes towards food.

5. **Mindful Preparation**: Mindful Eating begins before the food even reaches the plate. It involves mindful preparation of meals, including selecting fresh, whole foods, and taking the time to cook with care and attention. Practitioners may also cultivate gratitude for the nourishment provided by the food.

6. **Eating with Intention**: Mindful Eating encourages individuals to eat with intention and purpose, choosing foods that nourish their body, mind, and spirit. Practitioners may consider the nutritional value of their food choices and how they will support their overall health and

well-being.

7. **Awareness of Emotional Eating**: Mindful Eating also involves bringing awareness to emotional eating patterns and habits. Practitioners learn to recognize when they are eating in response to emotions such as stress, boredom, or sadness, and to explore alternative ways of coping with these emotions.

8. **Cultivating Gratitude**: Mindful Eating fosters a sense of gratitude for the abundance of food available and the individuals involved in the food production process, from farmers and growers to cooks and servers. Practitioners may take a moment to express gratitude before and after eating, acknowledging the interconnectedness of all beings.

By practicing Mindful Eating, individuals can cultivate a healthier and more balanced relationship with food, enhance their enjoyment of meals, and promote overall well-being. It offers an opportunity to slow down, savor the simple pleasures of eating, and nourish the body, mind, and spirit.

29

29

Mindful Communication

Mindful Communication is a practice that involves bringing awareness, intention, and presence to our interactions with others. It draws upon principles of mindfulness, compassion, and active listening to foster deeper connections, understanding, and harmony in our relationships. Here's an overview of Mindful Communication:

1. **Present Moment Awareness**: Mindful Communication begins with being fully present in the moment during conversations and interactions. Practitioners cultivate awareness of their thoughts, feelings, and physical sensations as well as the words and actions of others.

2. **Non-Judgmental Listening**: Mindful Communication emphasizes non-judgmental listening, where individuals listen to others without jumping to conclusions, interrupting, or formulating responses in their minds. They practice open-mindedness and receptivity, allowing space for the speaker to express themselves fully.

3. **Empathetic Understanding**: Practitioners of Mindful Communication seek to understand the perspective, emotions, and needs of others with empathy and compassion. They put themselves in the shoes of the speaker, acknowledging their feelings and validating their experiences without judgment or criticism.

4. **Clear and Authentic Expression**: Mindful Communication involves

expressing oneself authentically and clearly, using language that is honest, respectful, and non-harmful. Practitioners strive to communicate their thoughts, feelings, and intentions with clarity and transparency, avoiding passive-aggressive or manipulative communication patterns.

5. **Mindful Pause**: Before responding to others, practitioners of Mindful Communication take a mindful pause to reflect on their thoughts and emotions. They consider the impact of their words and actions on others and choose their responses consciously, rather than reacting impulsively or defensively.

6. **Compassionate Feedback**: When offering feedback or constructive criticism, individuals practicing Mindful Communication do so with compassion and kindness. They focus on the behavior or issue at hand rather than attacking the person's character, and they offer suggestions for improvement in a supportive and non-threatening manner.

7. **Cultivating Patience and Tolerance**: Mindful Communication requires patience and tolerance, especially in challenging or conflictual situations. Practitioners remain calm and composed, even when faced with disagreements or differing opinions, and they seek to resolve conflicts with understanding and mutual respect.

8. **Mindful Use of Technology**: In today's digital age, Mindful Communication also extends to our interactions online and through technology. Practitioners strive to use digital communication mindfully, avoiding distractions, misunderstandings, and misinterpretations, and fostering meaningful connections in virtual spaces.

By practicing Mindful Communication, individuals can enhance the quality of their relationships, improve their emotional intelligence, and contribute to a more harmonious and compassionate society. It offers an opportunity to cultivate deeper connections, understanding, and empathy in our interactions with others, both in-person and online.

Mindful Communication is an approach to interpersonal interaction that emphasizes awareness, presence, and compassion in all forms of communication. It draws upon principles of mindfulness, encouraging individuals to communicate with greater clarity, empathy, and understanding. Here's an overview of Mindful Communication:

1. **Present Moment Awareness**: Mindful Communication begins with cultivating present moment awareness in conversations. Practitioners strive to be fully present and attentive to the person they are communicating with, letting go of distractions and preconceived notions.

2. **Non-Judgmental Listening**: Mindful Communication involves non-judgmental listening, where individuals listen without immediately jumping to conclusions or forming judgments. Practitioners strive to listen with an open mind and heart, giving the speaker their full attention and respect.

3. **Empathetic Understanding**: Mindful Communication emphasizes empathetic understanding, where individuals seek to understand the thoughts, feelings, and perspectives of others. Practitioners practice active listening, reflecting back what they hear and validating the speaker's experience.

4. **Speaking with Clarity and Intention**: Mindful Communication encourages individuals to speak with clarity and intention, choosing their words mindfully and expressing themselves authentically. Practitioners strive to communicate honestly and transparently, avoiding gossip, manipulation, or passive-aggressive behavior.

5. **Cultivating Compassion**: Mindful Communication is infused with compassion and kindness towards oneself and others. Practitioners recognize the inherent worth and dignity of every person and seek to communicate with respect, empathy, and goodwill.

6. **Mindful Conflict Resolution**: Mindful Communication provides tools for resolving conflicts and disagreements peacefully and constructively. Practitioners learn to navigate challenging conversations with patience, understanding, and a willingness to find common ground.

7. **Awareness of Body Language and Nonverbal Cues**: Mindful Communication involves paying attention to nonverbal cues, such as body language, facial expressions, and tone of voice. Practitioners are mindful

of their own body language and the signals they are sending, as well as being attuned to the nonverbal cues of others.

8. **Practicing Mindful Speech**: Mindful Communication extends beyond verbal interactions to include written communication, social media interactions, and other forms of expression. Practitioners are mindful of the impact of their words and strive to communicate in ways that promote understanding, connection, and harmony.

By practicing Mindful Communication, individuals can cultivate deeper connections, build stronger relationships, and foster a culture of empathy, respect, and understanding in their personal and professional lives. It offers an opportunity to communicate with greater awareness, authenticity, and compassion, leading to more meaningful and fulfilling interactions with others.

30

30

Meditation and Creativity

Meditation and Creativity are deeply intertwined, with meditation practices often serving as a powerful tool for enhancing creativity and fostering inspiration. Here's an exploration of the relationship between meditation and creativity:

1. **Quieting the Mind**: Meditation helps quieten the incessant chatter of the mind, creating space for creative insights to arise. By calming the mental noise and reducing distractions, meditation allows individuals to tap into the wellspring of creativity within.

2. **Accessing the Subconscious**: Through meditation, individuals can access the deeper layers of the subconscious mind where creativity resides. By quieting the conscious mind and entering a state of relaxation, meditation can unlock new ideas, perspectives, and solutions that may not be readily accessible in the waking state.

3. **Enhancing Focus and Concentration**: Meditation strengthens the ability to focus and sustain attention, essential skills for creative work. By training the mind to remain present and undistracted, meditation helps individuals immerse themselves fully in the creative process, leading to greater productivity and innovation.

4. **Cultivating Mindfulness and Awareness**: Mindfulness practices, such as mindfulness meditation, cultivate present moment awareness

and heightened sensory perception. By becoming more attuned to the present moment, individuals can experience life with greater clarity and receptivity, sparking creative inspiration from the simplest of experiences.

5. **Stimulating Imagination**: Meditation stimulates the imagination and fosters a sense of inner exploration and creativity. By exploring the depths of consciousness through meditation, individuals can tap into the boundless realm of imagination and creativity, where ideas flow freely and innovation flourishes.

6. **Reducing Self-Criticism and Judgement**: Meditation helps individuals cultivate self-compassion and acceptance, reducing the inner critic that often stifles creativity. By letting go of self-judgment and perfectionism, individuals can embrace experimentation and playfulness, fostering a more open and expansive creative mindset.

7. **Connecting with Inner Wisdom**: Meditation enables individuals to connect with their inner wisdom and intuition, a rich source of creative inspiration. By quietening the mind and tuning into the intuitive guidance that arises from within, individuals can access fresh ideas, novel solutions, and creative breakthroughs.

8. **Creating Space for Reflection and Integration**: Meditation creates space for reflection and integration, allowing individuals to process their experiences and insights more deeply. By incorporating meditation into their creative practice, individuals can refine their ideas, clarify their vision, and bring greater depth and authenticity to their creative work.

Overall, the practice of meditation offers a wealth of benefits for enhancing creativity, from quieting the mind and accessing the subconscious to cultivating mindfulness and intuition. By integrating meditation into their creative process, individuals can unlock new levels of inspiration, innovation, and artistic expression, leading to more fulfilling and impactful creative endeavors.

Meditation and creativity are deeply intertwined, with meditation practices often serving as powerful tools for enhancing and stimulating creative thinking, innovation, and artistic expression. Here's how meditation can fuel creativity:

1. **Accessing the Subconscious Mind**: Meditation allows individuals to access deeper layers of consciousness, including the subconscious mind, where creativity often resides. By quieting the conscious mind and reducing mental chatter, meditation creates space for new ideas, insights, and inspiration to emerge from the subconscious.

2. **Cultivating Presence and Awareness**: Meditation cultivates presence and awareness, helping individuals become more attuned to their inner thoughts, emotions, and sensory experiences. This heightened awareness can fuel creativity by providing a deeper understanding of one's inner world and external surroundings, leading to new perspectives and creative breakthroughs.

3. **Enhancing Focus and Concentration**: Meditation strengthens the ability to focus and sustain attention, which is essential for creative endeavors that require deep concentration and immersion. By training the mind to stay present and focused, meditation enables individuals to delve into creative projects with clarity, precision, and flow.

4. **Reducing Mental Blocks and Self-Criticism**: Meditation helps to reduce mental blocks, self-doubt, and self-criticism that can inhibit creativity. By cultivating a non-judgmental attitude and acceptance of one's thoughts and emotions, meditation creates a supportive inner environment conducive to free expression and experimentation.

5. **Stimulating Divergent Thinking**: Certain meditation practices, such as mindfulness meditation, have been shown to stimulate divergent thinking—the ability to generate multiple creative solutions to a problem. By fostering a flexible and open-minded approach to problem-solving, meditation encourages creative thinking and innovation.

6. **Exploring the Creative Process**: Meditation provides an opportunity to explore the creative process itself, from inspiration and ideation to implementation and refinement. Through meditation, individuals can gain insights into their creative strengths, preferences, and areas for

growth, enhancing their overall creative practice.

7. **Connecting with Collective Consciousness**: Some meditation practices involve connecting with a sense of collective consciousness or universal creativity. By tapping into this deeper reservoir of creative energy, individuals may experience a sense of inspiration, interconnectedness, and shared creativity with others.

8. **Fostering Resilience and Adaptability**: Creativity often requires resilience and adaptability in the face of challenges, setbacks, and uncertainty. Meditation helps individuals develop resilience by cultivating qualities such as patience, perseverance, and equanimity, enabling them to navigate the ups and downs of the creative process with greater ease and grace.

Overall, meditation serves as a powerful ally in the pursuit of creativity, offering a pathway to deeper self-awareness, expanded consciousness, and enhanced creative expression. By integrating meditation into their creative practice, individuals can unlock new levels of inspiration, innovation, and artistic fulfillment.

31

31

Meditation for Stress Management

Meditation is a powerful tool for managing stress and promoting overall well-being. By calming the mind, relaxing the body, and fostering a sense of inner peace, meditation can help individuals reduce the negative effects of stress and cultivate resilience in the face of life's challenges. Here's how meditation can be used for stress management:

1. **Relaxation Response**: Meditation activates the body's relaxation response, which counteracts the stress response triggered by the sympathetic nervous system. Through deep breathing, progressive muscle relaxation, and mindfulness techniques, meditation induces a state of physical and mental relaxation, reducing tension and promoting a sense of calmness.

2. **Reduced Cortisol Levels**: Chronic stress can lead to elevated levels of cortisol, a hormone associated with the body's stress response. Research has shown that meditation can lower cortisol levels, helping to mitigate the harmful effects of chronic stress on the body and mind.

3. **Mindfulness-Based Stress Reduction (MBSR)**: Mindfulness meditation, as taught in programs like Mindfulness-Based Stress Reduction (MBSR), emphasizes non-judgmental awareness of present-moment experiences. By cultivating mindfulness, individuals learn to observe their thoughts, emotions, and bodily sensations with acceptance and

equanimity, reducing reactivity and enhancing resilience to stress.

4. **Stress Reduction Techniques**: Meditation incorporates a variety of stress reduction techniques, such as deep breathing exercises, body scan meditations, guided imagery, and progressive muscle relaxation. These techniques help individuals release physical tension, quiet the mind, and promote relaxation on both a physiological and psychological level.

5. **Enhanced Emotional Regulation**: Meditation strengthens the capacity for emotional regulation, enabling individuals to respond to stressors with greater composure and clarity. By observing their thoughts and emotions without attachment or judgment, practitioners develop a greater sense of emotional balance and resilience in the face of adversity.

6. **Improved Cognitive Functioning**: Chronic stress can impair cognitive functioning, leading to difficulties with concentration, memory, and decision-making. Meditation has been shown to improve cognitive function by enhancing attention, working memory, and executive functioning, thereby helping individuals cope more effectively with stressors in their lives.

7. **Enhanced Self-Compassion**: Meditation fosters self-compassion, which is essential for managing stress and promoting mental well-being. By cultivating a kind and compassionate attitude towards oneself, individuals can reduce self-criticism, perfectionism, and negative self-talk, fostering greater resilience and emotional well-being.

8. **Daily Practice**: Consistent meditation practice is key for effective stress management. Even just a few minutes of meditation each day can have profound benefits for reducing stress and promoting relaxation. By incorporating meditation into their daily routine, individuals can build resilience and cultivate a greater sense of inner peace and well-being over time.

In summary, meditation is a valuable tool for managing stress and promoting overall health and well-being. By incorporating meditation into their daily lives, individuals can cultivate greater resilience, emotional balance, and inner peace, enabling them to navigate life's challenges with greater ease and grace.

Meditation is widely recognized as an effective tool for managing stress and promoting relaxation, offering a holistic approach to reducing the physiological and psychological effects of stress on the body and mind. Here's how meditation can help with stress management:

1. **Relaxation Response**: Meditation triggers the body's relaxation response, which counteracts the physiological effects of stress, such as increased heart rate, elevated blood pressure, and shallow breathing. By inducing a state of deep relaxation, meditation helps to calm the nervous system and promote a sense of calm and well-being.

2. **Reduced Cortisol Levels**: Chronic stress can lead to elevated levels of the stress hormone cortisol, which can have harmful effects on physical and mental health. Meditation has been shown to reduce cortisol levels in the body, helping to alleviate the negative impact of stress on the body's systems.

3. **Mind-Body Connection**: Meditation cultivates awareness of the mind-body connection, allowing individuals to observe and understand how stress manifests in their thoughts, emotions, and physical sensations. By developing this awareness, individuals can learn to respond to stress in a more skillful and adaptive manner, rather than reacting automatically.

4. **Improved Emotional Regulation**: Meditation enhances emotional regulation by increasing mindfulness and self-awareness. Practitioners learn to observe their emotions without judgment and respond to them with greater equanimity and compassion. This can help prevent stress from escalating into overwhelming feelings of anxiety, anger, or frustration.

5. **Enhanced Resilience**: Regular meditation practice builds resilience to stress by strengthening the mind's capacity to cope with challenges and adversity. By cultivating qualities such as patience, acceptance, and inner strength, individuals become better equipped to navigate stressful situations with greater ease and adaptability.

6. **Better Sleep Quality**: Stress often disrupts sleep patterns, leading to difficulty falling asleep, staying asleep, or experiencing restful sleep.

Meditation promotes relaxation and reduces the activation of the body's stress response, helping individuals to achieve better sleep quality and wake up feeling more refreshed and rejuvenated.

7. **Increased Self-Care**: Meditation encourages self-care and self-compassion, empowering individuals to prioritize their well-being and make healthier lifestyle choices. By carving out time for meditation each day, individuals create space for self-reflection, self-care practices, and stress-reducing activities that nourish the body, mind, and spirit.

8. **Greater Sense of Control**: Stress often arises from feelings of powerlessness or lack of control over one's circumstances. Meditation helps individuals reclaim a sense of control by shifting their focus from external stressors to internal resources and strengths. By connecting with a deeper sense of inner peace and resilience, individuals can face stressors with greater confidence and empowerment.

Overall, meditation offers a comprehensive approach to stress management, addressing the underlying causes of stress while promoting relaxation, resilience, and emotional well-being. By integrating meditation into their daily routine, individuals can cultivate a healthier relationship with stress and live with greater ease, balance, and vitality.

32

32

Meditation for Better Sleep

Meditation can be a powerful tool for improving sleep quality and promoting restful, rejuvenating sleep. By calming the mind, reducing stress, and promoting relaxation, meditation can help individuals prepare for sleep and address common sleep disturbances. Here's how meditation can support better sleep:

1. **Relaxation Response**: Meditation induces the relaxation response, a state of deep relaxation that counteracts the body's stress response. By practicing meditation before bedtime, individuals can calm the nervous system, release tension, and create conditions conducive to falling asleep and staying asleep throughout the night.

2. **Reduced Anxiety and Stress**: Anxiety and stress are common contributors to sleep problems, such as difficulty falling asleep or staying asleep. Meditation helps to reduce anxiety and stress by promoting mindfulness, fostering a sense of inner calm, and encouraging a non-reactive attitude towards worrisome thoughts and feelings.

3. **Mindfulness-Based Stress Reduction (MBSR)**: Mindfulness meditation, a key component of MBSR, has been shown to improve sleep quality by reducing rumination, worry, and pre-sleep arousal. By practicing mindfulness techniques, such as focused attention on the breath or body scan meditation, individuals can cultivate present moment awareness

and let go of thoughts that interfere with sleep.

4. **Deep Relaxation Techniques**: Certain meditation practices, such as progressive muscle relaxation or guided imagery, can promote deep relaxation of the body and mind, facilitating the transition to sleep. By systematically releasing tension from the body and visualizing peaceful, calming scenes, individuals can create an optimal environment for sleep.

5. **Improved Sleep Hygiene**: Meditation can support healthy sleep habits and routines by promoting awareness of sleep hygiene practices. Practitioners may incorporate meditation into their bedtime routine, alongside other activities such as dimming lights, avoiding screens, and creating a comfortable sleep environment conducive to relaxation and restful sleep.

6. **Regulation of Circadian Rhythms**: Regular meditation practice can help regulate circadian rhythms, the internal biological clock that governs sleep-wake cycles. By establishing a consistent meditation routine, individuals can reinforce natural sleep-wake patterns and promote more regular, restorative sleep.

7. **Mindful Breathing for Sleep Onset**: Mindful breathing exercises can be particularly helpful for promoting sleep onset, or the ability to fall asleep quickly and easily. By focusing on slow, deep breathing and observing the sensations of the breath, individuals can calm the mind, quiet racing thoughts, and prepare for sleep.

8. **Increased Awareness of Sleep Patterns**: Meditation cultivates awareness of one's sleep patterns, including sleep quality, duration, and factors that may impact sleep. By paying attention to how meditation affects sleep and making adjustments as needed, individuals can optimize their meditation practice to better support restful sleep.

Overall, meditation offers a natural and effective approach to improving sleep quality and promoting overall well-being. By integrating meditation into their bedtime routine and cultivating mindfulness throughout the day, individuals can create the conditions for better sleep and wake up feeling refreshed, energized, and ready to face the day ahead.

Meditation can be a powerful tool for improving sleep quality and promoting restful, rejuvenating rest. By calming the mind, reducing stress, and promoting relaxation, meditation creates an optimal internal environment conducive to falling asleep and staying asleep. Here's how meditation can help improve sleep:

1. **Relaxation Response**: Meditation triggers the body's relaxation response, which counters the physiological effects of stress and promotes a state of deep relaxation. By calming the nervous system and reducing tension in the body, meditation prepares the mind and body for restful sleep.

2. **Stress Reduction**: Stress and anxiety are common culprits of sleep disturbances, making it difficult to fall asleep or stay asleep throughout the night. Meditation helps to reduce stress by calming the mind, soothing the nervous system, and promoting a sense of inner peace and tranquility.

3. **Mindfulness for Insomnia**: Mindfulness meditation, in particular, has been shown to be effective in treating insomnia and improving sleep quality. By cultivating present-moment awareness and non-judgmental acceptance of thoughts and sensations, mindfulness meditation helps individuals break free from rumination and worries that can interfere with sleep.

4. **Deep Relaxation**: Certain meditation techniques, such as body scan meditation or progressive muscle relaxation, promote deep relaxation by systematically releasing tension from the body. By scanning the body and consciously relaxing each muscle group, individuals can prepare their bodies for a restful night's sleep.

5. **Calming the Mind**: Racing thoughts and mental chatter can keep individuals awake at night, making it difficult to quiet the mind and drift off to sleep. Meditation teaches individuals to observe their thoughts without attachment or judgment, allowing them to let go of worries and concerns and enter a state of mental calmness and serenity.

6. **Breath Awareness**: Breath-focused meditation practices, such as

mindful breathing or deep belly breathing, can help individuals relax and unwind before bedtime. By focusing on the sensations of the breath and cultivating slow, deep breathing patterns, individuals can activate the body's relaxation response and prepare for sleep.

7. **Establishing a Bedtime Routine**: Incorporating meditation into a bedtime routine signals to the body that it's time to wind down and prepare for sleep. By consistently practicing meditation before bed, individuals establish a cue for relaxation and create a calming ritual that promotes better sleep habits.

8. **Improving Sleep Hygiene**: Meditation supports overall sleep hygiene by promoting healthy lifestyle habits that contribute to better sleep, such as maintaining a consistent sleep schedule, creating a comfortable sleep environment, and avoiding stimulants like caffeine or electronics before bedtime.

By integrating meditation into their bedtime routine, individuals can create the ideal conditions for restful, rejuvenating sleep, allowing them to wake up feeling refreshed, energized, and ready to tackle the day ahead.

33

33

Mental Health Benefits of Meditation

Meditation offers a wide range of mental health benefits, promoting emotional well-being, resilience, and overall psychological health. Here are some of the key mental health benefits of meditation:

1. **Stress Reduction**: Meditation is renowned for its ability to reduce stress levels by triggering the body's relaxation response. By calming the nervous system and reducing the production of stress hormones like cortisol, meditation promotes a sense of inner peace and tranquility.

2. **Anxiety Relief**: Meditation helps individuals manage anxiety by cultivating present-moment awareness and reducing rumination and worry. Mindfulness meditation, in particular, teaches individuals to observe their thoughts without judgment, allowing them to break free from patterns of anxious thinking.

3. **Improved Mood**: Regular meditation practice has been shown to improve mood and emotional well-being. By promoting the release of feel-good neurotransmitters like serotonin and dopamine, meditation can lift mood, reduce feelings of depression, and enhance overall emotional resilience.

4. **Enhanced Self-Awareness**: Meditation cultivates self-awareness by encouraging individuals to observe their thoughts, emotions, and sensa-

tions with curiosity and non-judgmental acceptance. This increased self-awareness enables individuals to identify and respond to their mental and emotional needs more skillfully.

5. **Greater Emotional Regulation**: Meditation enhances emotional regulation by increasing mindfulness and equanimity. Practitioners learn to recognize and manage their emotions more effectively, reducing reactivity and impulsivity and fostering a greater sense of emotional balance and stability.

6. **Improved Concentration and Focus**: Meditation strengthens the ability to concentrate and sustain attention, which can benefit overall cognitive function and productivity. By training the mind to stay present and focused, meditation enhances cognitive skills such as memory, attention, and problem-solving.

7. **Reduced Symptoms of PTSD**: Meditation has shown promise in reducing symptoms of post-traumatic stress disorder (PTSD) by helping individuals process traumatic experiences and manage associated symptoms such as hypervigilance, intrusive thoughts, and emotional distress.

8. **Enhanced Resilience**: Meditation builds resilience by strengthening the mind's capacity to cope with adversity and bounce back from setbacks. By cultivating qualities such as patience, acceptance, and inner strength, meditation empowers individuals to navigate life's challenges with greater ease and adaptability.

9. **Improved Sleep Quality**: Meditation promotes better sleep by calming the mind, reducing stress, and promoting relaxation. By incorporating meditation into a bedtime routine, individuals can create the ideal conditions for restful, rejuvenating sleep.

10. **Greater Overall Well-Being**: Ultimately, meditation promotes greater overall well-being by fostering a sense of inner peace, contentment, and connection. By nurturing the mind-body-spirit connection, meditation supports holistic health and encourages individuals to live with greater presence, purpose, and fulfillment.

Overall, meditation offers a holistic approach to mental health and well-being, empowering individuals to cultivate greater resilience, emotional balance, and inner peace in their lives.

Meditation offers a wide range of mental health benefits, promoting emotional well-being, resilience, and overall psychological wellness. Here are some of the key mental health benefits of meditation:

1. **Stress Reduction**: One of the most well-known benefits of meditation is its ability to reduce stress levels. By calming the mind, soothing the nervous system, and promoting relaxation, meditation helps individuals manage stress more effectively and cope with life's challenges with greater ease.

2. **Anxiety Relief**: Meditation has been shown to be effective in reducing symptoms of anxiety disorders, including generalized anxiety disorder, social anxiety disorder, and panic disorder. By promoting a sense of inner calm and tranquility, meditation helps individuals alleviate anxious thoughts and feelings.

3. **Improved Mood**: Regular meditation practice can enhance mood and emotional well-being by regulating mood-related neurotransmitters and promoting feelings of happiness and contentment. Meditation cultivates a sense of inner peace and equanimity, helping individuals navigate the ups and downs of life with greater emotional resilience.

4. **Depression Management**: Meditation has been found to be beneficial in managing symptoms of depression, including low mood, sadness, and loss of interest in activities. By fostering self-awareness, acceptance, and self-compassion, meditation helps individuals break free from negative thought patterns and cultivate a more positive outlook on life.

5. **Enhanced Emotional Regulation**: Meditation enhances emotional regulation by increasing mindfulness and self-awareness. Practitioners learn to observe their emotions without judgment and respond to them with greater equanimity and compassion. This helps prevent emotional reactivity and promotes a sense of emotional balance and stability.

6. **Increased Focus and Concentration**: Meditation strengthens the

ability to focus and sustain attention, which can improve cognitive function and productivity. By training the mind to stay present and focused, meditation enhances concentration skills and mental clarity, making it easier to stay on task and accomplish goals.

7. **Mindfulness and Self-Awareness**: Meditation cultivates mindfulness, or present-moment awareness, which helps individuals become more attuned to their thoughts, feelings, and bodily sensations. By developing self-awareness, individuals can identify and address underlying issues contributing to mental health challenges, leading to greater self-understanding and personal growth.

8. **Better Sleep Quality**: Meditation promotes relaxation and reduces the activation of the body's stress response, making it easier to fall asleep and stay asleep throughout the night. By calming the mind and body before bedtime, meditation improves sleep quality and helps individuals wake up feeling refreshed and rejuvenated.

Overall, meditation offers a holistic approach to mental health and well-being, addressing the underlying causes of mental health challenges while promoting resilience, self-awareness, and emotional balance. By integrating meditation into their daily routine, individuals can experience profound benefits for their mental health and overall quality of life.

34

34

Physical Health Benefits

Meditation offers a variety of physical health benefits that contribute to overall well-being and vitality. Here are some of the key physical health benefits of meditation:

1. **Stress Reduction**: Meditation is well-known for its ability to reduce stress levels, which in turn can have a positive impact on physical health. By calming the nervous system and promoting relaxation, meditation helps lower levels of stress hormones like cortisol, which are associated with a range of health issues, including high blood pressure, heart disease, and weakened immune function.

2. **Lower Blood Pressure**: Regular meditation practice has been linked to lower blood pressure levels. By promoting relaxation and reducing stress, meditation helps improve blood flow and vascular function, which can lead to lower blood pressure readings and reduced risk of cardiovascular disease.

3. **Heart Health**: Meditation can have a positive impact on heart health by reducing risk factors associated with heart disease, such as high blood pressure, inflammation, and oxidative stress. Studies have shown that meditation may improve cardiovascular health markers, including cholesterol levels, triglycerides, and markers of arterial stiffness.

4. **Pain Management**: Meditation has been found to be effective in

managing chronic pain conditions, such as back pain, arthritis, and migraines. By increasing mindfulness and awareness of bodily sensations, meditation can help individuals cope with pain more effectively and reduce reliance on pain medications.

5. **Improved Immune Function**: Meditation has been shown to enhance immune function by reducing inflammation and strengthening the body's natural defense mechanisms. By reducing stress and promoting relaxation, meditation helps regulate immune responses and enhance the activity of immune cells, which can help protect against infections and illness.

6. **Better Sleep Quality**: Meditation promotes relaxation and reduces the activation of the body's stress response, making it easier to fall asleep and stay asleep throughout the night. By calming the mind and body before bedtime, meditation improves sleep quality and helps individuals wake up feeling refreshed and rejuvenated.

7. **Digestive Health**: Stress can have a negative impact on digestive health, leading to issues like indigestion, irritable bowel syndrome (IBS), and inflammation in the gut. Meditation helps reduce stress levels and promote relaxation, which can have a beneficial effect on digestive function and alleviate symptoms of digestive disorders.

8. **Enhanced Respiratory Function**: Certain meditation techniques, such as deep breathing exercises, can improve respiratory function and lung capacity. By promoting slow, deep breathing patterns, meditation enhances oxygenation of the blood, reduces respiratory rate, and improves lung function, leading to better respiratory health overall.

Overall, meditation offers a holistic approach to physical health, addressing the interconnectedness of mind and body to promote overall well-being and vitality. By integrating meditation into their daily routine, individuals can experience profound benefits for their physical health and quality of life.

n addition to its well-known mental health benefits, meditation also offers numerous advantages for physical health. Here are some of the key physical health benefits of meditation:

1. **Stress Reduction**: Chronic stress can have detrimental effects on physical health, including increased risk of heart disease, high blood pressure, and weakened immune function. Meditation helps to counteract the effects of stress by triggering the body's relaxation response, lowering cortisol levels, and promoting a state of deep relaxation.

2. **Lower Blood Pressure**: Meditation has been shown to lower blood pressure in individuals with hypertension or prehypertension. By promoting relaxation and reducing stress, meditation helps to dilate blood vessels, improve circulation, and lower blood pressure levels, reducing the risk of cardiovascular disease.

3. **Improved Heart Health**: Regular meditation practice is associated with improved heart health and a reduced risk of heart disease. Meditation promotes relaxation, lowers blood pressure, and reduces inflammation in the body, all of which contribute to a healthier cardiovascular system and a lower risk of heart attack and stroke.

4. **Enhanced Immune Function**: Meditation has been found to boost immune function and increase the body's resistance to infections and illnesses. By reducing stress and inflammation in the body, meditation supports immune system function, helping to fight off pathogens and keep the body healthy and resilient.

5. **Pain Management**: Meditation can be effective in managing chronic pain conditions, such as arthritis, fibromyalgia, and migraines. By promoting relaxation and reducing the perception of pain, meditation helps individuals cope with pain more effectively and improve their overall quality of life.

6. **Better Sleep Quality**: Meditation promotes relaxation and reduces arousal, making it easier to fall asleep and stay asleep throughout the night. By calming the mind and body before bedtime, meditation improves sleep quality and helps individuals wake up feeling refreshed and rejuvenated.

7. **Improved Respiratory Function**: Certain meditation techniques, such as deep breathing exercises and mindfulness of breath, can improve respiratory function and lung capacity. By promoting slow, deep

breathing patterns, meditation enhances oxygenation of the blood and strengthens the respiratory muscles, leading to better lung health and overall respiratory function.

8. **Enhanced Digestive Health**: Meditation has been shown to improve digestive health and alleviate symptoms of gastrointestinal disorders, such as irritable bowel syndrome (IBS) and acid reflux. By reducing stress and promoting relaxation, meditation helps to regulate digestion, reduce inflammation in the gut, and improve overall digestive function.

Overall, meditation offers a wide range of physical health benefits, supporting overall well-being and vitality. By integrating meditation into their daily routine, individuals can experience profound improvements in their physical health, leading to a healthier, happier life.

35

35

Emotional and Spiritual Benefits of Meditation

Meditation offers a wealth of emotional and spiritual benefits, nurturing inner peace, personal growth, and a deeper connection to oneself and the world around us. Here are some of the key emotional and spiritual benefits of meditation:

1. **Inner Peace and Calmness**: Meditation cultivates a sense of inner peace and tranquility by quieting the mind and soothing the nervous system. Regular meditation practice helps individuals develop a greater sense of calmness and equanimity, even in the face of life's challenges and uncertainties.

2. **Stress Reduction**: Meditation is a powerful tool for managing stress and reducing its impact on our emotional well-being. By promoting relaxation, reducing cortisol levels, and fostering a state of deep relaxation, meditation helps individuals cope with stress more effectively and maintain emotional balance.

3. **Emotional Resilience**: Regular meditation practice strengthens emotional resilience, helping individuals bounce back from setbacks and adversity with greater ease and grace. By cultivating mindfulness, self-awareness, and self-compassion, meditation empowers individuals to

navigate the ups and downs of life with greater emotional strength and flexibility.

4. **Increased Happiness and Well-Being**: Meditation is associated with greater levels of happiness and overall well-being. By promoting positive emotions such as gratitude, compassion, and joy, meditation helps individuals cultivate a more optimistic outlook on life and experience greater satisfaction and fulfillment.

5. **Self-Discovery and Personal Growth**: Meditation is a journey of self-discovery and personal growth, inviting individuals to explore the depths of their inner being and uncover their true nature. Through meditation, individuals gain insight into their thoughts, emotions, and beliefs, fostering greater self-awareness and self-understanding.

6. **Enhanced Creativity and Intuition**: Meditation stimulates creativity and intuition by quieting the mind and tapping into the subconscious mind. By accessing deeper levels of consciousness, meditation allows individuals to tap into their creative potential and receive intuitive insights and inspiration.

7. **Spiritual Awakening**: Meditation is a spiritual practice that can lead to profound experiences of spiritual awakening and enlightenment. By transcending the ego and connecting with the higher self or universal consciousness, meditation opens the door to spiritual insights, inner wisdom, and a deeper understanding of the nature of reality.

8. **Connection to Something Greater**: Meditation fosters a sense of connection to something greater than oneself, whether it be the universe, nature, or a higher power. By cultivating a sense of interconnectedness and oneness with all beings, meditation deepens our appreciation for the sacredness of life and our place in the cosmic order.

Overall, meditation offers a transformative journey of emotional and spiritual growth, leading to greater peace, joy, and fulfillment in life. By integrating meditation into their daily routine, individuals can experience profound benefits for their emotional well-being and spiritual evolution.

Meditation is not only beneficial for mental and physical health but also offers profound advantages for emotional and spiritual well-being. Here are some of the key emotional and spiritual benefits of meditation:

1. **Emotional Regulation**: Meditation enhances emotional regulation by increasing mindfulness and self-awareness. Practitioners learn to observe their emotions without judgment and respond to them with greater equanimity and compassion. This helps prevent emotional reactivity and promotes a sense of emotional balance and stability.

2. **Stress Reduction and Resilience**: Meditation helps individuals manage stress more effectively and develop greater resilience in the face of life's challenges. By promoting relaxation, reducing cortisol levels, and calming the nervous system, meditation empowers individuals to navigate stressful situations with greater ease and adaptability.

3. **Increased Positive Emotions**: Regular meditation practice is associated with increased feelings of happiness, joy, and gratitude. By cultivating present-moment awareness and non-attachment to thoughts and emotions, meditation helps individuals appreciate the simple pleasures of life and find beauty and meaning in everyday experiences.

4. **Greater Self-Compassion**: Meditation fosters self-compassion and self-acceptance, enabling individuals to cultivate a kind and nurturing relationship with themselves. Practitioners learn to treat themselves with the same kindness and compassion they would offer to a friend, leading to greater self-esteem and emotional well-being.

5. **Enhanced Intuition and Insight**: Meditation opens the door to deeper levels of intuition and insight, allowing individuals to tap into their inner wisdom and guidance. By quieting the mind and listening to the inner voice of intuition, meditation helps individuals make decisions aligned with their values and purpose, leading to greater clarity and fulfillment.

6. **Connection with Others**: Meditation fosters a sense of interconnectedness and compassion towards others, promoting empathy, understanding, and kindness in relationships. By cultivating a heart-centered approach to interactions, meditation helps individuals cultivate deeper connections with others and foster a sense of community and belonging.

7. **Spiritual Growth and Awakening**: Meditation is a powerful tool for spiritual growth and awakening, offering a pathway to transcendence and self-realization. Through meditation, individuals can connect with a deeper sense of purpose and meaning, explore existential questions, and experience profound states of unity, oneness, and interconnectedness with the universe.

8. **Cultivation of Gratitude and Forgiveness**: Meditation cultivates gratitude and forgiveness, helping individuals let go of past grievances and cultivate a sense of appreciation for life's blessings. By practicing gratitude and forgiveness, individuals experience greater emotional freedom, inner peace, and spiritual fulfillment.

Overall, meditation offers a holistic approach to emotional and spiritual well-being, supporting individuals on their journey towards greater self-awareness, inner peace, and personal growth. By integrating meditation into their daily routine, individuals can experience profound emotional and spiritual benefits, leading to a more fulfilling and meaningful life.

36

36

Building Self-Awareness Through Meditation

Self-awareness is the foundation of personal growth, emotional intelligence, and well-being. Meditation is a powerful tool for cultivating self-awareness, allowing individuals to deepen their understanding of themselves and their inner world. Here's how meditation can help build self-awareness:

1. **Mindfulness of Thoughts and Emotions**: Meditation teaches individuals to observe their thoughts and emotions with non-judgmental awareness. By becoming more mindful of the contents of their mind, individuals gain insight into their thought patterns, beliefs, and emotional reactions, fostering greater self-awareness.

2. **Body Awareness**: Meditation involves tuning into bodily sensations and becoming more aware of the physical sensations present in the body. By paying attention to sensations such as tension, discomfort, or relaxation, individuals develop a greater understanding of the mind-body connection and how emotions manifest in the body.

3. **Identifying Patterns and Triggers**: Through meditation, individuals can identify recurring patterns of thought, behavior, and emotional triggers. By observing these patterns with curiosity and compassion,

166

individuals gain insight into the underlying causes of their thoughts, emotions, and behaviors, leading to greater self-awareness and personal growth.

4. **Exploring Core Values and Beliefs**: Meditation provides an opportunity to explore core values, beliefs, and priorities. By reflecting on what matters most to them and aligning their actions with their values, individuals deepen their understanding of themselves and gain clarity about their goals and aspirations.

5. **Observing the Inner Critic**: Meditation helps individuals recognize and disengage from the inner critic—the voice of self-judgment and self-doubt. By observing the inner critic with mindfulness and compassion, individuals can cultivate greater self-acceptance and self-compassion, fostering a more positive and nurturing inner dialogue.

6. **Developing Emotional Intelligence**: Meditation enhances emotional intelligence by increasing awareness of one's own emotions and the emotions of others. By observing and accepting their emotions without judgment, individuals develop greater emotional resilience, empathy, and interpersonal skills.

7. **Deepening Introspection and Reflection**: Meditation provides a space for introspection and self-reflection, allowing individuals to explore their inner landscape with curiosity and openness. By carving out time for quiet reflection, individuals can deepen their self-awareness and gain clarity about their values, goals, and priorities.

8. **Cultivating Presence and Authenticity**: Meditation fosters a sense of presence and authenticity, enabling individuals to show up fully in each moment and live with greater integrity and alignment with their true selves. By cultivating mindfulness and self-acceptance, individuals can live more authentically and intentionally, leading to greater fulfillment and well-being.

Overall, meditation is a powerful tool for building self-awareness and deepening understanding of oneself. By integrating meditation into their daily routine, individuals can cultivate greater self-awareness, emotional intelligence, and authenticity, leading to a more meaningful and fulfilling life. Meditation is a powerful tool for cultivating self-awareness, or the ability to observe and understand one's thoughts, emotions, and behaviors without judgment. Here's how meditation can help build self-awareness:

1. **Observing the Mind**: Through meditation, individuals learn to observe the activity of their mind without getting caught up in its fluctuations. By sitting quietly and observing the flow of thoughts, emotions, and sensations, individuals develop greater insight into their mental patterns and tendencies.

2. **Recognizing Thought Patterns**: Meditation helps individuals recognize recurring thought patterns and habits of mind that may be influencing their behavior and emotions. By becoming aware of these patterns, individuals can begin to challenge and reframe negative or limiting beliefs, leading to greater mental clarity and emotional well-being.

3. **Exploring Emotional Responses**: Meditation encourages individuals to explore their emotional responses with curiosity and compassion. By observing emotions as they arise and dissipate without attachment or aversion, individuals develop greater emotional resilience and a deeper understanding of the underlying causes of their feelings.

4. **Cultivating Mindfulness**: Mindfulness meditation, in particular, is focused on developing present-moment awareness and non-judgmental acceptance of one's thoughts, emotions, and sensations. By practicing mindfulness, individuals become more attuned to their internal experiences and develop greater clarity and insight into their inner world.

5. **Body Awareness**: Meditation often involves body scan techniques, where individuals systematically bring their attention to different parts of the body. By cultivating body awareness, individuals become more in tune with physical sensations and learn to identify areas of tension or discomfort that may be linked to underlying emotional or psychological stressors.

6. **Identifying Triggers and Reactions**: Through meditation, individuals

learn to identify triggers that evoke strong emotional reactions and automatic responses. By recognizing these triggers, individuals can pause and respond thoughtfully rather than reacting impulsively, leading to more skillful and adaptive behavior.

7. **Developing Self-Compassion**: Meditation fosters self-compassion by encouraging individuals to cultivate kindness and acceptance towards themselves. By observing their thoughts and emotions with a compassionate attitude, individuals develop greater self-acceptance and learn to treat themselves with kindness and understanding.

8. **Reflecting on Values and Intentions**: Meditation provides an opportunity for individuals to reflect on their values, priorities, and intentions in life. By connecting with their deepest aspirations and desires, individuals gain clarity about what truly matters to them and can align their actions and behaviors accordingly.

Overall, meditation is a powerful practice for building self-awareness and fostering personal growth. By cultivating mindfulness, exploring internal experiences, and developing greater insight into oneself, individuals can cultivate a deeper sense of self-awareness and lead more authentic, purposeful lives.

selflove
gratitude
heart
Mind
passion
music
nature
attract right
planet
@HelloVivek

37

37

Enhancing Emotional Intelligence through Meditation

Emotional intelligence (EI) is the ability to recognize, understand, and manage one's own emotions, as well as to recognize, understand, and influence the emotions of others. Meditation is a powerful tool for enhancing emotional intelligence by cultivating self-awareness, self-regulation, empathy, and social skills. Here's how meditation can help enhance emotional intelligence:

1. **Self-Awareness**: Meditation cultivates self-awareness by encouraging individuals to observe their thoughts, emotions, and bodily sensations without judgment. By practicing mindfulness meditation, individuals become more attuned to their internal experiences and gain insight into their emotional patterns and triggers.

2. **Self-Regulation**: Meditation helps individuals develop greater self-regulation by teaching them to respond to emotions in a calm, thoughtful manner rather than reacting impulsively. Through meditation, individuals learn to observe their emotional responses without getting swept away by them, allowing for more skillful and adaptive behavior.

3. **Empathy**: Meditation promotes empathy by fostering a deeper understanding of one's own emotions and experiences, which in turn enhances

the ability to empathize with others. By cultivating compassion and kindness towards oneself, individuals naturally extend these qualities towards others, leading to greater empathy and understanding in interpersonal interactions.

4. **Emotion Regulation**: Meditation teaches individuals how to regulate their emotions more effectively by cultivating mindfulness and self-awareness. By observing emotions as they arise and dissipate without attachment or aversion, individuals develop greater emotional resilience and learn to respond to challenging emotions with equanimity and compassion.

5. **Stress Management**: Meditation is a powerful tool for managing stress, which is essential for maintaining emotional balance and well-being. By triggering the body's relaxation response and reducing cortisol levels, meditation helps individuals cope with stress more effectively and prevents it from overwhelming their emotional state.

6. **Improved Communication**: Meditation enhances communication skills by promoting active listening, empathy, and non-verbal communication. By cultivating presence and attentiveness through meditation, individuals become better listeners and more attuned to the emotions and needs of others, leading to more effective and meaningful communication.

7. **Conflict Resolution**: Meditation fosters conflict resolution skills by promoting empathy, understanding, and non-judgmental communication. By practicing mindfulness and compassion towards oneself and others, individuals can navigate conflicts more skillfully and find mutually beneficial resolutions.

8. **Cultivation of Positive Relationships**: Meditation strengthens interpersonal relationships by fostering qualities such as empathy, compassion, and authenticity. By cultivating a deeper understanding of oneself and others, individuals can build stronger, more authentic connections based on trust, mutual respect, and emotional intimacy.

Overall, meditation is a powerful tool for enhancing emotional intelligence and promoting greater emotional well-being, resilience, and interpersonal effectiveness. By integrating meditation into their daily routine, individuals can develop the skills and qualities necessary for navigating life's challenges with grace, wisdom, and compassion.

Emotional intelligence refers to the ability to recognize, understand, and manage one's own emotions, as well as to recognize, understand, and influence the emotions of others. Meditation is a valuable tool for enhancing emotional intelligence by promoting self-awareness, self-regulation, empathy, and social skills.   Here's how meditation can help enhance emotional intelligence:

1. **Self-Awareness**: Meditation cultivates self-awareness by encouraging individuals to observe their thoughts, emotions, and sensations without judgment. Through practices such as mindfulness meditation, individuals develop greater awareness of their internal experiences and gain insight into their emotional patterns and triggers.

2. **Self-Regulation**: Meditation helps individuals regulate their emotions more effectively by teaching them to respond to challenging situations with calmness and clarity rather than impulsivity or reactivity. By practicing techniques such as deep breathing or loving-kindness meditation, individuals learn to regulate their emotional responses and maintain a sense of inner balance and equanimity.

3. **Empathy**: Meditation fosters empathy by encouraging individuals to cultivate compassion and understanding towards themselves and others. Through practices such as loving-kindness meditation, individuals develop a sense of connection and empathy towards others, recognizing their shared humanity and common experiences.

4. **Social Skills**: Meditation enhances social skills by promoting communication, empathy, and interpersonal understanding. By cultivating mindfulness and presence in social interactions, individuals become better listeners, communicators, and collaborators, fostering positive and supportive relationships with others.

5. **Conflict Resolution**: Meditation provides individuals with tools for resolving conflicts and disagreements peacefully and constructively. By cultivating a sense of calmness and equanimity through meditation, individuals can approach conflict situations with greater clarity and empathy, leading to more effective and mutually beneficial resolutions.

6. **Stress Management**: Meditation is effective in managing stress and promoting emotional resilience, which are essential components of emotional intelligence. By reducing stress levels and promoting relaxation, meditation helps individuals maintain emotional balance and cope with challenging situations more effectively.

7. **Emotional Awareness in Others**: Meditation enhances individuals' ability to recognize and understand the emotions of others by increasing their own emotional awareness. Through practices such as mindfulness meditation, individuals become more attuned to subtle emotional cues and nonverbal communication, allowing them to respond empathetically and effectively to the emotions of others.

8. **Adaptability and Flexibility**: Meditation promotes adaptability and flexibility in response to changing circumstances and challenges. By cultivating a mindset of acceptance and non-attachment through meditation, individuals become more resilient in the face of adversity and more open to learning and growth.

Overall, meditation is a powerful tool for enhancing emotional intelligence, promoting self-awareness, self-regulation, empathy, and social skills. By incorporating meditation into their daily routine, individuals can develop a deeper understanding of themselves and others, leading to more fulfilling relationships, improved communication, and greater overall well-being.

38

<h1 style="text-align:center">38</h1>

Cultivating Gratitude through Meditation

Gratitude is a powerful practice that can enhance well-being, promote positive emotions, and foster a sense of fulfillment and contentment in life. Meditation offers a pathway to cultivate gratitude by training the mind to focus on the present moment and cultivate appreciation for the blessings and abundance in one's life. Here's how meditation can help cultivate gratitude:

1. **Mindfulness of the Present Moment**: Meditation promotes mindfulness, or present-moment awareness, which is essential for cultivating gratitude. By focusing on the present moment without judgment, individuals become more attuned to the richness and beauty of their immediate experience, leading to greater appreciation for life's simple pleasures.

2. **Gratitude Meditation**: Gratitude meditation is a specific form of meditation that involves reflecting on the things, people, and experiences for which one is grateful. By dedicating time each day to consciously cultivate feelings of gratitude, individuals can strengthen their capacity for appreciation and foster a positive outlook on life.

3. **Counting Blessings**: Meditation can involve a practice of counting blessings, where individuals mentally list the things they are grateful for. By acknowledging and expressing gratitude for the abundance in

their lives, individuals shift their focus away from scarcity and cultivate a mindset of abundance and appreciation.

4. **Loving-Kindness Meditation**: Loving-kindness meditation, also known as Metta meditation, involves sending well-wishes of love, compassion, and gratitude to oneself and others. By cultivating feelings of kindness and gratitude towards oneself and others, individuals expand their capacity for love and appreciation.

5. **Gratitude Journaling**: Meditation can be combined with journaling as a way to deepen the practice of gratitude. By writing down the things they are grateful for each day, individuals reinforce feelings of appreciation and create a record of the positive aspects of their lives to reflect upon.

6. **Mindful Reflection**: Meditation encourages individuals to reflect mindfully on their experiences, both positive and negative. By reframing challenging situations through the lens of gratitude, individuals can find meaning and growth even in difficult circumstances, leading to greater resilience and emotional well-being.

7. **Appreciation of Nature**: Meditation often involves connecting with nature and the natural world, which can evoke feelings of awe, wonder, and gratitude. By spending time in nature and appreciating the beauty and interconnectedness of all living beings, individuals cultivate a deeper sense of gratitude for the world around them.

8. **Living with Gratitude**: Ultimately, meditation helps individuals embody the practice of gratitude in their daily lives, leading to a more positive and fulfilling existence. By integrating gratitude into their thoughts, words, and actions, individuals can experience greater happiness, resilience, and overall well-being.

Overall, meditation offers a powerful pathway to cultivate gratitude, leading to greater happiness, fulfillment, and appreciation for the richness of life. By incorporating gratitude practices into their meditation routine, individuals can foster a positive outlook and embrace life with open hearts and minds.

Meditation is a powerful practice for cultivating gratitude, or the ability to recognize and appreciate the positive aspects of life, even in the midst of challenges or difficulties. Here's how meditation can help cultivate gratitude:

1. **Mindfulness of the Present Moment**: Meditation encourages individuals to cultivate mindfulness, or present-moment awareness, which helps them recognize and appreciate the simple pleasures of life that often go unnoticed. By focusing attention on the present moment, individuals become more attuned to the beauty and richness of their surroundings, fostering a sense of gratitude for the abundance of life.

2. **Gratitude Meditation**: Gratitude meditation is a specific meditation practice designed to cultivate feelings of gratitude and appreciation. During gratitude meditation, individuals reflect on the things they are grateful for, such as relationships, experiences, or qualities about themselves. By intentionally focusing on gratitude, individuals strengthen neural pathways associated with positive emotions and foster a more grateful outlook on life.

3. **Counting Blessings**: Another meditation technique for cultivating gratitude is the practice of counting blessings or keeping a gratitude journal. Individuals can set aside time each day to reflect on the things they are grateful for and write them down in a journal. By regularly acknowledging and recording their blessings, individuals cultivate a habit of gratitude and shift their focus towards the positive aspects of life.

4. **Shift in Perspective**: Meditation helps individuals shift their perspective from one of scarcity and lack to one of abundance and appreciation. By training the mind to focus on what is present rather than what is absent, individuals develop a more optimistic and grateful outlook on life, even in the face of challenges or adversity.

5. **Awareness of Impermanence**: Meditation encourages individuals to recognize the impermanent nature of life and appreciate each moment as it arises. By cultivating awareness of impermanence, individuals develop a deeper appreciation for the fleeting beauty of life and the preciousness of each experience, fostering a sense of gratitude for the

present moment.

6. **Connection with Others**: Meditation fosters a sense of interconnectedness and compassion towards others, which in turn cultivates gratitude for the support and kindness of others. By recognizing the contributions of others to their lives, individuals develop a sense of appreciation and gratitude for the relationships and connections that enrich their lives.

7. **Fostering Contentment**: Meditation promotes contentment and inner peace by encouraging individuals to find happiness and fulfillment in the present moment rather than constantly striving for more. By cultivating contentment, individuals develop a sense of gratitude for what they have rather than focusing on what they lack, leading to greater overall satisfaction and well-being.

8. **Spreading Kindness and Generosity**: Meditation encourages individuals to cultivate kindness and generosity towards others, which fosters a sense of gratitude for the opportunity to make a positive impact in the world. By spreading kindness and generosity, individuals create a ripple effect of gratitude and appreciation that enriches their own lives as well as the lives of others.

Overall, meditation is a powerful practice for cultivating gratitude, fostering a deeper appreciation for life's blessings, and promoting a more joyful and fulfilling way of being. By incorporating gratitude into their daily meditation practice, individuals can cultivate a more positive and grateful outlook on life, leading to greater happiness, resilience, and well-being.

39

39

Finding Inner Peace through Meditation

Meditation is a powerful practice for finding inner peace, or a state of calmness, tranquility, and harmony within oneself. Here's how meditation can help individuals cultivate inner peace:

1. **Quieting the Mind**: Meditation involves quieting the mind and slowing down the constant stream of thoughts, worries, and distractions that can disturb inner peace. By practicing techniques such as mindfulness meditation or focused attention meditation, individuals learn to let go of mental chatter and find stillness and clarity within.

2. **Letting Go of Attachment**: Meditation encourages individuals to let go of attachment to external circumstances or outcomes and find peace within themselves. By cultivating an attitude of non-attachment and acceptance, individuals can find inner peace regardless of the ups and downs of life.

3. **Cultivating Presence**: Meditation cultivates presence, or the ability to fully engage with the present moment without judgment or resistance. By focusing attention on the here and now, individuals can let go of worries about the past or future and find peace in the present moment.

4. **Acceptance and Surrender**: Meditation fosters acceptance and surrender, allowing individuals to accept things as they are and surrender to the flow of life. By letting go of the need to control or resist, individuals

can find inner peace and trust in the unfolding of life's journey.

5. **Connecting with Inner Wisdom**: Meditation provides individuals with access to their inner wisdom and intuition, guiding them towards a deeper sense of inner peace and clarity. By quieting the mind and listening to the inner voice of intuition, individuals can tap into a source of guidance and wisdom that brings a sense of peace and alignment.

6. **Cultivating Compassion and Forgiveness**: Meditation fosters compassion and forgiveness towards oneself and others, leading to greater inner peace and emotional healing. By cultivating kindness and compassion through practices such as loving-kindness meditation, individuals can release resentments and find peace in the heart.

7. **Mind-Body Connection**: Meditation promotes awareness of the mind-body connection, helping individuals recognize how their thoughts and emotions affect their physical state. By cultivating relaxation and calmness through meditation, individuals can release tension and find a sense of inner peace in the body.

8. **Living in Alignment with Values**: Meditation encourages individuals to live in alignment with their values and priorities, leading to greater inner peace and fulfillment. By connecting with their deepest aspirations and desires, individuals can live authentically and find peace in living a life that is true to themselves.

Overall, meditation is a powerful practice for finding inner peace, fostering a sense of calmness, tranquility, and harmony within oneself. By incorporating meditation into their daily routine, individuals can cultivate a deeper sense of inner peace and live with greater ease, balance, and contentment.

Meditation is a powerful practice for finding inner peace, a state of calmness, tranquility, and harmony within oneself. Here's how meditation can help individuals find inner peace:

1. **Quieting the Mind**: Meditation helps individuals quiet the incessant chatter of the mind by focusing attention on the present moment. Through practices such as mindfulness meditation, individuals learn to

observe their thoughts without attachment or judgment, allowing the mind to gradually settle into a state of stillness and tranquility.

2. **Letting Go of Stress and Tension**: Meditation promotes relaxation and reduces the activation of the body's stress response, helping individuals let go of tension and stress stored in the body. By practicing techniques such as deep breathing or progressive muscle relaxation, individuals release physical and mental tension, creating space for inner peace to arise.

3. **Cultivating Acceptance and Equanimity**: Meditation fosters acceptance and equanimity by encouraging individuals to embrace each moment as it arises, without resistance or attachment. Through practices such as loving-kindness meditation, individuals cultivate a sense of openness and acceptance towards themselves and others, fostering inner peace and emotional well-being.

4. **Connecting with the Present Moment**: Meditation cultivates mindfulness, or present-moment awareness, which helps individuals connect with the richness and beauty of the present moment. By focusing attention on the here and now, individuals let go of worries about the past or future, experiencing a sense of peace and contentment in the present moment.

5. **Developing Gratitude and Appreciation**: Meditation encourages individuals to cultivate gratitude and appreciation for the simple pleasures of life. By focusing attention on the things they are grateful for, individuals shift their perspective towards the positive aspects of life, fostering a sense of inner peace and fulfillment.

6. **Connecting with Nature**: Meditation can be practiced outdoors, allowing individuals to connect with the natural world and experience a sense of peace and harmony with their surroundings. By immersing themselves in nature, individuals tap into the healing power of the earth, fostering a deeper sense of inner peace and connection with all living beings.

7. **Letting Go of Attachments and Expectations**: Meditation teaches individuals to let go of attachments and expectations, allowing them

to experience life with greater ease and flow. By releasing the need to control outcomes or cling to desires, individuals cultivate a sense of inner peace and acceptance of whatever arises in the present moment.

8. **Cultivating Compassion and Loving-Kindness**: Meditation fosters compassion and loving-kindness towards oneself and others, promoting a sense of interconnectedness and unity. By cultivating a heart-centered approach to life, individuals experience greater inner peace and fulfillment, knowing that they are connected to all beings in the universe.

Overall, meditation is a powerful practice for finding inner peace, fostering a deep sense of calmness, tranquility, and harmony within oneself. By incorporating meditation into their daily routine, individuals can experience greater peace of mind, emotional well-being, and spiritual fulfillment.

40

40

Achieving Mindfulness in Everyday Life

Mindfulness is the practice of paying attention to the present moment with openness, curiosity, and acceptance. While meditation is often associated with mindfulness, the goal is to integrate mindfulness into everyday life. Here are some ways to achieve mindfulness in your daily activities:

1. **Mindful Breathing**: Incorporate mindful breathing into your daily routine by taking a few moments to focus on your breath. Whether you're commuting, waiting in line, or taking a break, pause and bring your attention to the sensation of your breath entering and leaving your body. This simple practice can help anchor you in the present moment and calm the mind.

2. **Mindful Eating**: Practice mindful eating by paying attention to the sensory experience of eating, such as the taste, texture, and smell of your food. Slow down and savor each bite, noticing the flavors and sensations as you chew. Eating mindfully can enhance your enjoyment of food and promote healthier eating habits.

3. **Mindful Walking**: Take time to practice mindful walking by bringing awareness to each step you take. Feel the ground beneath your feet, notice the movement of your body, and observe your surroundings with curiosity. Walking mindfully can help you feel more grounded, present,

and connected to the world around you.

4. **Mindful Listening**: Practice mindful listening in your interactions with others by giving them your full attention without judgment or distraction. Listen with empathy and curiosity, tuning into both the words and the emotions behind them. Mindful listening can deepen your connections with others and enhance your communication skills.

5. **Mindful Work**: Bring mindfulness to your work by approaching tasks with focus, intention, and presence. Take breaks to pause and check in with yourself, noticing any tension or stress in your body and allowing yourself to reset. Mindful work can increase productivity, creativity, and overall job satisfaction.

6. **Mindful Technology Use**: Use technology mindfully by setting boundaries and being intentional about how you engage with digital devices. Take breaks from screens, limit multitasking, and practice awareness of your online activities. Mindful technology use can help reduce stress and improve your relationship with technology.

7. **Mindful Self-Care**: Prioritize self-care activities that promote mindfulness, such as yoga, meditation, or journaling. Take time each day to nurture your physical, emotional, and mental well-being, honoring your needs and boundaries. Mindful self-care can help you feel more balanced, resilient, and grounded in your daily life.

8. **Mindful Reflection**: Dedicate time for mindful reflection at the end of each day to review your experiences and insights. Journaling or meditation can be helpful practices for processing your thoughts and emotions, gaining clarity, and setting intentions for the day ahead. Mindful reflection can deepen your understanding of yourself and your life journey.

By incorporating mindfulness into your daily activities, you can cultivate a greater sense of presence, awareness, and fulfillment in every moment. Remember that mindfulness is a practice that requires patience, persistence, and self-compassion, so be gentle with yourself as you explore and deepen your mindfulness journey.

Mindfulness is the practice of paying deliberate attention to the present moment without judgment. Integrating mindfulness into everyday life can lead to greater awareness, emotional balance, and overall well-being. Here are some ways to achieve mindfulness in everyday life:

1. **Start with Intention**: Begin each day with the intention to be mindful and present in all your activities. Set the intention to pay attention to your thoughts, emotions, and sensations as you go about your day.

2. **Practice Mindful Breathing**: Take moments throughout the day to pause and focus on your breath. Notice the sensations of breathing— the rise and fall of your chest, the sensation of air entering and leaving your nostrils. This simple practice can anchor you in the present moment and bring a sense of calmness and clarity.

3. **Engage Fully in Activities**: Whether you're eating, walking, or washing dishes, bring full awareness to the activity at hand. Notice the sensations, smells, and tastes involved. Engaging fully in each activity can transform ordinary moments into opportunities for mindfulness and presence.

4. **Use Mindful Reminders**: Set reminders or cues throughout your day to bring you back to the present moment. This could be a sound, a visual cue, or simply a moment of pause to check in with yourself and notice your surroundings.

5. **Practice Gratitude**: Cultivate a sense of gratitude by noticing and appreciating the small moments of joy and beauty in your life. Take time each day to reflect on what you're grateful for, whether it's a kind gesture from a friend or the warmth of the sun on your skin.

6. **Acceptance and Non-Judgment**: Practice accepting things as they are without judgment or resistance. Notice when your mind starts to label experiences as good or bad and gently bring your focus back to the present moment without attaching to the judgments.

7. **Mindful Communication**: Practice mindful communication by listening fully to others without interrupting or formulating your response. Notice your own reactions and emotions as you engage in conversation and respond with kindness and empathy.

8. **Mindful Movement**: Incorporate mindfulness into your movement practices, such as yoga, tai chi, or walking meditation. Pay attention to the sensations in your body as you move and notice how it feels to be fully present in each moment.

9. **Mindful Eating**: Bring awareness to your eating habits by paying attention to the colors, textures, and flavors of your food. Eat slowly and savor each bite, noticing how your body responds to nourishment.

10. **Reflect on Your Day**: Take time at the end of each day to reflect on your experiences with curiosity and kindness. Notice any moments of mindfulness or areas where you could bring more awareness tomorrow.

By incorporating these practices into your daily life, you can cultivate greater mindfulness and presence, leading to a deeper sense of connection, peace, and fulfillment in everyday experiences.

41

41

Continuing Your Meditation Journey

Embarking on a meditation journey is just the beginning of a lifelong practice that can bring profound benefits to your physical, mental, and emotional well-being. Here are some tips for continuing and deepening your meditation practice:

1. **Set Realistic Goals**: Reflect on your meditation journey so far and set realistic goals for what you hope to achieve in the future. Whether it's cultivating greater inner peace, reducing stress, or deepening self-awareness, having clear intentions can guide your practice.

2. **Consistency is Key**: Establish a consistent meditation routine by setting aside time each day for practice. Whether it's first thing in the morning, during your lunch break, or before bed, find a time that works for you and commit to showing up for your practice regularly.

3. **Explore Different Techniques**: There are many meditation techniques to explore, from mindfulness and loving-kindness to breathwork and visualization. Experiment with different practices to find what resonates with you and brings you the most benefit.

4. **Join a Community**: Consider joining a meditation group or community to connect with like-minded individuals and gain support for your practice. Whether it's an in-person group or an online community, sharing your experiences with others can enhance your motivation and

deepen your understanding of meditation.

5. **Seek Guidance**: If you're feeling stuck or unsure about your meditation practice, seek guidance from a meditation teacher or mentor. They can offer personalized advice, answer your questions, and provide encouragement to help you navigate any challenges that arise.

6. **Stay Open-Minded**: Approach your meditation practice with an open mind and a spirit of curiosity. Be willing to explore new techniques, ideas, and experiences without judgment or attachment to specific outcomes.

7. **Practice Self-Compassion**: Be gentle and compassionate with yourself as you continue your meditation journey. Remember that meditation is a practice, not a performance, and it's okay to have ups and downs along the way. Treat yourself with kindness and patience as you navigate the challenges and joys of meditation.

8. **Integrate Mindfulness into Daily Life**: Extend the benefits of meditation beyond your formal practice sessions by incorporating mindfulness into your daily life. Practice bringing mindful awareness to everyday activities such as walking, eating, and communicating with others.

9. **Cultivate Gratitude**: Cultivate gratitude for your meditation practice and the benefits it brings to your life. Take time to reflect on the positive changes you've experienced and express gratitude for the opportunity to deepen your understanding of yourself and the world around you.

10. **Stay Committed**: Finally, stay committed to your meditation practice even when it feels challenging or you encounter obstacles along the way. Trust in the process and know that each moment of presence and awareness brings you closer to greater peace, clarity, and well-being.

By continuing to nurture your meditation practice with patience, dedication, and openness, you can experience profound transformation and growth on your journey towards greater self-awareness, inner peace, and fulfillment.

Embarking on a meditation journey is just the beginning of a lifelong practice that can bring profound benefits to your life. Here are some tips for continuing and deepening your meditation practice:

1. **Consistency is Key**: Make meditation a regular part of your daily routine by setting aside a specific time each day for practice. Consistency is crucial for building momentum and deepening your meditation skills over time.

2. **Explore Different Techniques**: There are many meditation techniques to explore, from mindfulness meditation to loving-kindness meditation to breathwork and more. Experiment with different techniques to find what resonates most with you and keeps your practice fresh and engaging.

3. **Set Realistic Expectations**: Understand that meditation is a practice, not a destination. Be patient with yourself and set realistic expectations for your progress. Some days your mind may be more restless than others, and that's okay. Simply showing up and practicing is what matters most.

4. **Find Support and Community**: Seek out like-minded individuals who share your interest in meditation. Join a meditation group or community where you can connect with others, share experiences, and receive support and encouragement on your journey.

5. **Cultivate Mindfulness in Daily Life**: Extend the benefits of meditation beyond your formal practice sessions by incorporating mindfulness into your everyday activities. Practice bringing awareness to simple tasks like walking, eating, or washing dishes, and notice how mindfulness enhances your experience of these activities.

6. **Deepen Your Understanding**: Take time to deepen your understanding of meditation by reading books, attending workshops, or listening to talks by experienced meditation teachers. Cultivating knowledge and insight can enrich your practice and inspire you to explore new avenues of meditation.

7. **Set Intentions for Growth**: Reflect on your meditation practice regularly and set intentions for growth and development. Whether it's cultivating more compassion, enhancing focus and concentration,

or deepening self-awareness, setting clear intentions can guide your practice and keep you motivated.

8. **Be Gentle with Yourself**: Meditation is a journey of self-discovery and growth, and it's natural to encounter challenges along the way. Be gentle with yourself and practice self-compassion as you navigate the ups and downs of your meditation journey.

9. **Stay Open-Minded and Curious**: Approach your meditation practice with an open mind and a spirit of curiosity. Stay open to new experiences and insights that arise during meditation, and be willing to explore different approaches and techniques as your practice evolves.

10. **Celebrate Your Progress**: Take time to acknowledge and celebrate your progress on your meditation journey. Whether it's noticing increased calmness and clarity in your mind or experiencing greater peace and contentment in your life, celebrate the positive changes that meditation brings.

Remember that meditation is a deeply personal practice, and your journey will be unique to you. Stay committed, stay curious, and above all, enjoy the journey of self-discovery and transformation that meditation offers.

Embarking on a meditation journey is just the beginning of a lifelong practice that can bring profound benefits to your life. Here are some tips for continuing and deepening your meditation practice:

1. **Consistency is Key**: Commit to practicing meditation regularly, even if it's just for a few minutes each day. Consistency is more important than duration, so aim to establish a daily meditation habit that you can maintain over time.

2. **Explore Different Techniques**: Experiment with different meditation techniques to find what works best for you. Whether it's mindfulness meditation, loving-kindness meditation, or guided imagery, there are many approaches to meditation, so explore and discover what resonates with you.

3. **Set Realistic Expectations**: Understand that meditation is a journey,

and progress may not always be linear. Be patient with yourself and set realistic expectations for your practice. It's okay to have days where your mind feels restless or distracted—simply observe without judgment and continue with your practice.

4. **Seek Guidance and Support**: Consider joining a meditation group or finding a meditation teacher to guide you on your journey. Having support and guidance from others can provide valuable insights and encouragement as you navigate the challenges and joys of meditation.

5. **Integrate Mindfulness into Daily Life**: Extend the benefits of meditation beyond your formal practice by incorporating mindfulness into your daily activities. Practice being present and fully engaged in whatever you're doing, whether it's eating, walking, or talking with a friend.

6. **Stay Open and Curious**: Approach your meditation practice with an open mind and a sense of curiosity. Be willing to explore new techniques, perspectives, and experiences as you deepen your understanding of yourself and the world around you.

7. **Cultivate Self-Compassion**: Be gentle and compassionate with yourself as you continue your meditation journey. There will be days when your mind feels scattered or your practice feels challenging—this is all part of the process. Treat yourself with kindness and understanding, just as you would a dear friend.

8. **Reflect on Your Progress**: Take time to reflect on your meditation practice and the changes you've noticed in yourself over time. Celebrate your achievements and milestones, no matter how small, and acknowledge the growth and transformation that meditation has brought into your life.

9. **Stay Inspired**: Seek inspiration from books, podcasts, or talks on meditation and mindfulness. Surround yourself with supportive resources that nourish your practice and inspire you to continue on your meditation journey.

10. **Trust the Process**: Trust that your meditation practice is unfolding exactly as it should, and have faith in the transformative power of

meditation to bring greater peace, clarity, and well-being into your life.

Remember that meditation is a lifelong journey of self-discovery and growth. Embrace the ups and downs, the challenges and breakthroughs, and trust in the process as you continue to deepen your meditation practice and cultivate greater presence, peace, and awareness in your life.